Woods Hole Daze

A Cape Cod Memoir

Phillip L. Pendergast

Riverhaven Books

www.RiverhavenBooks.com

The pieces contained within include stories from the author's experiences of the people and places of Woods Hole.

Published in the United States by Riverhaven Books,
www.RiverhavenBooks.com

Paperback ISBN: 978-1-951854-23-2

Front cover photo of Nobska Light by
Emily Ferguson, Land's Edge Photography

Back cover photo of author in Thailand by
Claudia Pendergast Dion

Back cover and interior layout by
Stephanie Blackman, Whitman, Massachusetts

Printed in the United States of America
by Country Press, Lakeville, Massachusetts

Table of Contents

Sunset over Eel Pond
Photo courtesy of Beth Colt at Woods Hole Inn

INTRODUCTION

Dear Reader;

I had the good fortune of growing up in Woods Hole, Massachusetts during the fifties and sixties. Woods Hole is a small village consisting of about 900 year-round residents. It is a beautiful place surrounded on three sides by water. Woods Hole is also most famous for its world-renowned research centers. The Marine Biological Laboratory (MBL) and Woods Hole Oceanographic Institution (WHOI) are located there. In fact, Doctor Robert Ballard, who discovered the sunken Titanic back in 1985, was from WHOI. Many scientists from all over the world come every summer sponsored by grants and fellowships to do research in the various labs at the MBL. Several scientists have gone on to win Nobel Prizes due to research done at Woods Hole. Also, many professors come each summer to teach graduate students courses in marine biology, embryology, entomology, and other courses. Despite this notoriety, many people only think of Woods Hole as the place to catch the ferry to Martha's Vineyard and Nantucket. At any rate, I would like to share with you some recollections about my years growing up in this quaint seaside village and scientific community.

Now that I find myself well into my third act, I felt that it was high time that I put pen to paper and write this memoir. This little book that you have in your hands is my attempt to share with you my recollections of growing up in Woods Hole.

My thought was that I should try to record these events while my mind is relatively keen and my memory is still in tact. In other words, I wanted to document these episodes while I'm still lucid and in possession of all my marbles.

Thus, you are in possession of a short memoir about a teenaged boy growing up on Cape Cod back when life was more innocent and people kinder. In those happy days, things moved along at a more leisurely pace. The internet, cell phones, Facebook, IPads, and text messages did not bombard our senses with distractions and noise 24/7. Days seemed to last longer then, and the summers seemed to go on forever.

I chose the word "Daze" in the title because, in hindsight, it appeared to me that my memories flowed back in a mystical, almost hazy form. Moreover, Woods Hole has always enjoyed a reputation as a quaint little village (750 souls back then) composed of many brilliant scientists and a cast of local characters who were known to march to their own drum. For these reasons, and many others, Woods Hole has always been viewed as a very unique, unconventional seaside community.

I have tried as best I could to record the following events as they actually did occur. In a few rare exceptions, I had to employ some dialogue of my own since I could not recall the exact words that were spoken. However, all the events portrayed here actually did take place. So, sit back in a comfy chair, pour yourself a glass of Merlo, and travel back in time with me and enjoy *Woods Hole Daze*.

*****

As I lay patiently in bed waiting for
Morpheus to embrace me, slowly drifting
into a state twixt consciousness and sleep…
A mosaic of memories begins to form in
my mind.
A kaleidoscope of images flood my brain
and I return once again to those Golden
Days of my youth.

Phillip Pendergast
September 2021

Pendergast Family Photo – Thanksgiving 1950

Left to right: Phillip L.Pendergast, Christine Pendergast, Claudia R. Pendergast, Claudia M. Pendergast Dion

DEDICATION

I would like to dedicate this memoir to the memory of my mother, Claudia Pendergast. My mother was a remarkable woman who lived a long and extraordinary life. She was a fiercely independent lady who lived her life on her own terms. By the time my mother was sixteen years old, both her parents had passed. After graduating from Marycliff Academy, she put herself through the Portia School of Law, now Suffolk University. She graduated in 1938. This was quite an accomplishment for a woman back in those days. She was in the process of studying for the Bar exam when she met my dad and got married. Even though she never practiced law, her knowledge from law school was useful during her long real estate career.

The following words are taken from the eulogy I gave at her memorial service.

CLAUDIA R. PENDERGAST

1915-2001

My mother moved to Woods Hole with her three children during the spring of 1951 after recently separating from my father. She was thirty-six years old, I was seven, Kate was five, and Chris was about six months old. I remember that we arrived in a black Model A Ford (We have a great picture of that.) We settled into a small bungalow that my mother had bought from a maiden aunt. The house was very small, with only one bedroom, no basement, and a floor central furnace as a source of heat. We converted an unheated porch into a second bedroom.

5 Park Street, Woods Hole, MA

I remember that we had very little room and basically no furniture to speak of. I also remember that Chris slept in a drawer for a while, although I'm sure she would deny this fact! Also, we didn't have a bathtub or shower in this cottage. Therefore, on Saturday nights, we would have our baths in the large kitchen sink. We used to call this "Squish night" because of the sound that the sponge made. We do happen to have a picture of Chris in the sink.

To remedy the lack of a full bathroom, my mother decided to expand to a full bathroom by herself. I remember very well holding the 2 by 4s while she hammered the nails into the plywood. The end result was a full bathroom with a stall shower. No more sink baths for us!

Mom was always very strict about us attending Mass every Sunday. Many times we would walk along the path at the end of Park Street and through the ballpark to this very church. Kate and I med our first confirmations here. Also, I was an altar boy here from age 10-15. By the way, the statue of Saint Jude to the right of the altar was donated by my mom 45 years ago. My mother had a very strong liking for Saint Jude since he was considered the Patron Saint of difficult circumstances.

Katie and I have great memories of growing up on Park Street in the early '50s. In fact, I would say that those years were some of the happiest years of my life in a lot of ways, and I wouldn't trade them for anything. Kate and I enjoyed riding our bikes to the MBL (Stoney) Beach and also "downtown" as we referred to the small center of Woods Hole. During all this time, Mom made sure we looked out for Chris, and we always did.

My mother was a very hard worker with a lot of energy and a great zest for life. She initially worked for someone who had a small real estate business, and she took over that business in 1950. She also ran the local Western Union service from that same little office. Back in those days, they used the tickertape machines, and one glued the tapes onto the Western Union blank pages.

Over the years, my mother built up a very large clientele of summer renters. Most of these people were distinguished scientists coming from all over the world to do research at the laboratories at Woods Hole. Whenever a scientist came to do research, or to teach grad students, his first call was to Claudia in hopes of obtaining housing. Somehow my mother was able to place all these people, even if it meant renting out a room in our house on Nobska Road where I grew up. Many of her clients were Nobel Prize winners who ended up buying their summer homes from my mother.

My mother enjoyed doing the summer rentals and making sure that the properties were cleaned, lawns mowed, and the utilities changed over. This was a very time consuming and labor-intensive process that involved coordinating a lot of service people with whom she established great rapport and respect. Many times, people would stop me on the street and remark to me what a hard worker she was and what an inspiration she was to them.

19 Nobska Road, Woods Hole, MA

Whenever Mom had any free time, one of her ways of "relaxing" was to buy an old house that needed work, totally rehab it, and then sell it. She was very clever at this and did all the painting and most of the carpentry herself. Charlotte Joseph, a local photographer and friend, would work with her on these projects. As a matter of fact, one of the houses she rehabbed is located just a few streets away from this church.

My mother was an adventurous person, so she bought a 16' speed boat with a 35-horsepower Evinrude motor. She really enjoyed riding the waves over to Tarpaulin Cove, Falmouth Harbor, and even Martha's Vineyard. She especially liked to sit on top of the driver's seat so she could see farther. Also, that way, she could control the steering wheel with her foot. This always worked out okay until one day she got caught in the rip-tide off Nobska Point. The sea was very choppy that day and she had a frightening experience when the boat almost capsized. Unfortunately, after that, she lost a lot of her enthusiasm for boating.

Mom was also a very accomplished golfer. In fact, she won a golf tournament in her 80th year. She belonged to three golf clubs, and she had many wonderful golfing adventures with her friend Wendy Forbes. Shortly before her death, Mom said, "Dear, if you do one of those talks about me, would you put something in it about me being a pretty good golfer."

My mother didn't swear, but she had a few humorous expressions when she got upset: "So help me Hannah." Kate and I never did learn who Hannah was. Another expression when she was exasperated was: "Good luck to you and the Red Sox." Actually, she was a big Red Sox fan and also an avid football fan. The day before she passed away, she wanted to make sure that she knew what time the Patriot's game started and whether the hospital TV was hooked up so she could watch it.

My mother was a very interesting person with a great intellect, boundless energy, and a dry sense of humor.

1. She was both an optimist and a realist.
2. She was a competitive athlete and a passionate friend.
3. She was a sharp businesswoman, but she was

scrupulously honest.

4. She was a very hard worker, but she also took time to enjoy her life and her family.

5. She was both a very public person and a very private person.

She was all these things and much more. But…most importantly…she was a wonderful mother and we all loved her.

*****

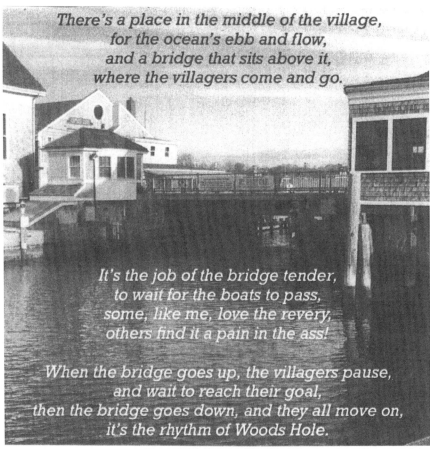

There's a place in the middle of the village,
for the ocean's ebb and flow,
and a bridge that sits above it,
where the villagers come and go.

It's the job of the bridge tender,
to wait for the boats to pass,
some, like me, love the revery,
others find it a pain in the ass!

When the bridge goes up, the villagers pause,
and wait to reach their goal,
then the bridge goes down, and they all move on,
it's the rhythm of Woods Hole.

Poem by Matthew Sheehan
Photo credit: Eel Pond Bridge

WOODS HOLE DAZE

a poem

Hot August morning.

Barefoot we walk to the beach.

Trying to stay on the white lines.

So hot asphalt doesn't burn our feet.

Up the hill we go.

Passing the lighthouse on our right.

We descend and Nobska Beach awaits.

Weather beaten bath houses – a raft offshore.

Bright sun reflects off the water.

Seagulls soar in the azure sky.

The perfume of pink beach roses.

HEAVEN

*****

HURRY! HURRY!

Too late!

Drawbridge goes up.

"Tourists, go home" appears once again in orange spray
paint.

Stuck in traffic at noontime.

A sloop leaves Eel Pond.

Slips through the narrow passage.

Heading out toward Vineyard Sound.

*****

We ride our bikes to *Stoney*.

Lay on our towels.

The smell of Coppertone.

Little kids make sandcastles.

We swim out to Paradise Rock.

Join the kids jumping off.

RING! RING!

The Ice Cream Man.

Two ice cream sandwiches for us.

Two blasts from the town horn – 4:30 already?

Time to bike home for supper.

*****

Night swim at Nobska.

Warm water.

Bioluminescence sparkles like a million tiny diamonds.

Swim out to raft.

Dive off twice.

Return to shore.

Short bike ride home.

Fireflies flash in the darkness.

The sound of crickets.

*****

SEPTEMBER:

Timid ripples caress the deserted shore.

Lifeguards gone – diving rafts removed.

Bathhouses forlorn and empty.

Summer cottages shuttered for the winter.

Phillip L. Pendergast

Tourists, research scientists, and their students
long since departed.
Just the locals now.
The sound of laughter on the beaches and streets has
evaporated.
SILENCE.
Indian summer has arrived and…
The feeling
Is
BITTERSWEET

Nobska Bathhouses

Photo credit: Claudia Pendergast Dion

GRANNY KIDDER

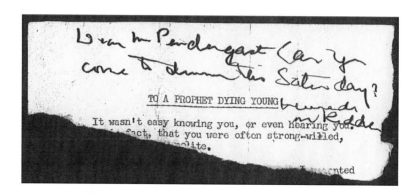

She was a tiny, bird-like little lady who probably weighed about a hundred pounds. She always wore her grey hair fashioned into a bun on the top of head. She was about five-feet, two-inches tall, but she appeared shorter due to her slump caused by severe osteoporosis. This posture caused her to appear to always looking for something she had lost on the ground. No one ever knew just how old she was, but it was assumed she was somewhere in her eighties. Her given name was Mariah Kidder, but she was known affectionately by many folks simply as "Granny" Kidder.

Granny was a familiar fixture during the summer months of the 1950s. Everybody knew that she was "down for the summer" when she drove into our small town center in her light blue, somewhat beat-up, '48 Ford. Since she was so tiny, she could barely see over her steering wheel. Her eyesight was not the best either, and she was a *terrible* driver. Everyone was on guard when her old Ford was spotted weaving down the main road and into town.

Granny's husband had died many years earlier. Now during the winter months she lived in a very nice apartment (I believe) on Fifth Avenue in New York City. However, during the summer she lived in a huge old house in Woods Hole, located right on Vineyard Sound, with about 200' of private beach front. Today that property would easily be worth about $4,000,000.00. Despite her wealth, Granny was very unassuming.

Granny Kidder had three or four grown children. She also had grandchildren….. a *lot* of them! One of her daughters and many of the grandkids lived with her in the large house during the summer months. In addition, a housekeeper and a cook also lived there. At any rate, it was indeed a full house.

Granny adored all her grandchildren, who ranged in age from 2 ½ years to their mid-twenties. Since the children were down for the summer and didn't know any of the local kids, Granny was always trying to round up some local teenagers to come over and play/party with her grandkids.

Granny was very resourceful and not the least discriminating. Sometimes when she went downtown, she would randomly invite some local kids to come to her house to meet and play with her grandkids. Frequently, on her four-mile drive to Falmouth, she would stop and pick up a couple of young kids hitchhiking. It was a different era then, but still a risky thing to do. After riding a few minutes, she would turn to her young passengers and say: "Would you like to go to a party?" The shocked young people often said: "Sure lady. Where is it?" She would then go on to tell them her name and address. Often times, the exact time was vague: "Oh, about 6:00PM this Saturday night. It's my granddaughter's birthday, and there will be a lot of young people there." Most of these hitchhikers didn't know anything about Mrs. Kidder or where she lived. Surprisingly, some of the invited kids *did* show up. I would have loved to have seen the expressions on their faces when they walked up her driveway.

I still smile when I remember one of those parties which I attended with my cousin, Paul. Wewere about seventeen years old that year and he was staying with me for the summer. Granny had run into Paul and me at the local post office and asked if we would like to come over that Saturday night for a party. I'm not sure, but I think it might have been one of those birthday parties for one of her grandchildren, because she told us to come over about 6:00PM and that there was no need to bring a present.

When Paul and I showed for the party, we mistakenly went to a side door that led into the kitchen. We knocked on the screen door and were greeted by a jovial maid. I asked her whether there was a party there that night and she said, "Honey, come on in. There's a party here every night. Follow me." The maid led us down a hallway and into a large dining room.

There was a long table with about twenty young people seated around it. Paul and I said "Hello" and took our seats.

The youngest kid was probably about ten and the oldest appeared to be in his mid-twenties. At any rate, I remember that there was a *very* unique assortment of people. I sat next to a preppy-looking guy about twenty years old, dressed in a white turtleneck, sports jacket, and chino pants, and wearing Bass Weegan loafers. Paul was sitting next to some kid about eighteen years old, sporting a tie-died t-shirt and ragged Dungaree shorts and his hair had been braided into some kind of ponytail. To complete the picture, he was wearing a pair of dirty sneakers and no socks.

"Hmmmmm," I thought. "Don't know him, but he looks familiar. Gotta be a native Woods Hole product for sure."

All the kids were polite and well mannered. The problem was that with such an eclectic group, most people had nothing in common with the person sitting next to them. Everyone tried to make some idle chit chat while waiting for the food to be served. Within ten minutes, the maid appeared and placed a big platter of roast beef at each end of the table. She then returned with bowls of mashed-potatoes and vegetables and set them about the table.

That seemed to do the trick! Everyone passed the bowls and platters and helped themselves to the feast. I don't remember much about the rest of that evening, but somehow we all seemed to succeed in having pleasant conversations with each other. We played several board games and the party broke up about 10:00PM. I do recall when I was about to leave, Granny was telling me that she was concerned because her granddaughter's boyfriend was leaving the next day to go into the service. Apparently, the granddaughter was broken-hearted and Mrs. Kidder was trying to console her.

On another occasion, Granny set up a party at the Landfall Restaurant in Woods Hole. It was another grandchild's birthday, and she had arranged the whole thing and paid for it in advance. I remember sitting next to a year-round kid from Woods Hole who was in my class at Lawrence High School in Falmouth.

I remember getting gas one day, at our only filling station in town. It was only twenty-five cents per gallon at that time. The owner was filling my car when he heard another car approaching and looked up. He said, "Oh, God. Here she comes again! The last time she was here, she backed up into one of my pumps. I cannot believe that she's still on the road." I followed his gaze and saw Granny Kidder coming down the one-way street at a good clip aiming right for the gas station. With a squeal of brakes, she came to an abrupt stop right next to the other pump.

Granny leaned out her window, smiled sweetly, and said, "Hi, Al. Would you fill me up with regular and check my tires?"

Al just smiled back and replied, "Sure thing, Mrs. Kidder. Just as soon as I finish with Phil here."

Now that I reflect back upon this incident, I wonder if Granny was unable to pass her driver's renewal test but was riding around with an expired license.

I guess my favorite Granny Kidder story would be her trip to our local *Package Store*. I was not there to observe this.

However, I knew the owner well, and he related the following to me. He told me that one afternoon Granny came in and purchased two cases of beer. The beer was bottled and the two cases were heavy. Granny was trying to lug the first case out to her car when the store owner told her to put the case down and he would do it for her. She accepted his offer and went to open her trunk. The man deposited the two cases in her trunk and closed the lid. Then he said, "Boy, Mrs. Kidder, you must be having a big party."

She quickly replied, "Oh, gracious no! It's not for me. It's for my grandchildren. They are too young to buy it for themselves, so I am buying it for them." Then she got in her car, closed the door and drove off. He just couldn't believe it!

And so ends my recollections of Granny Kidder. It was a simpler, more innocent time back then, and I remember her with fondness.

*****

WOODS HOLE SCHOOL

Woods Hole School is located at 24 School Street and abuts Eel Pond. The original structure was built in 1840 and only had two rooms. In 1885, it was expanded to a four-room schoolhouse. The building was added to the National Register of Historic Places in 2008.

I started to attend second grade there when we first moved to Woods Hole in 1950. I was seven years old. I remained at the school through grade five. Starting in 6th grade, students took Bus 8 to the Mullen Hall School in Falmouth, about 4 miles away. Grades 7–12 continued on in the newly built Falmouth High School. I remember Pick Wright, the bus driver. He was a huge man and always had to enter the bus sideways.

Woods Hole is a very small village, so often two small classes (6–10 students) were merged into one larger class. The teacher spent the first half of class time teaching one grade level. Then she would teach the second half of the class at the next grade level. During that time the first half of the class would be doing their homework.

I had many happy memories of this unique school. My classes were on the second floor. I well remember Mrs. Noreen Robinson, who I had for my last (5th grade) year. She was a tall, big-boned woman, and I thought that she was somewhat intimidating. She was also the school principal and very no-nonsense. She loved Peter Paul and Almond Joy chocolate bars.

10

Every so often she would give me, or another student, ten cents and send us down to the drug store to get her a bar.

School started at 9:00AM. There was an American flag in each classroom. Every day before class we stood and recited the Pledge of Allegiance. Then we recited a psalm. I think it was always the 23rd Psalm: *"The Lord is my shepherd…"* (I wish they still did this today.) Then we would sit down at our desks. The desks were those old-fashioned wooden ones with the chair attached. There was a wooden top that you could lift up. Also, there was a hole drilled in the top of each desk where an inkwell used to be. At noon we broke for lunch and recess. We would have our lunch and play on the playground. We would use the slides, swings, monkey bars, see-saw, and this kind of weird thing called a "Stride." Basically it was a tall metal pole with a series of chains hanging down. There was a hand bar at the end of each chain. You were supposed to grab the bar and run around the pole then swing out to the side. All in all, not a very safe amusement as you could get hit by a chain when someone suddenly dropped off. (That contraption is not there today.)

There was a large school bell located in the cupola on the roof. There was a long, thick rope that you had to pull down HARD to ring the bell. For some strange reason, only 4th graders were allowed this special privilege. At 1:00PM, the bell would be rung, indicating that recess was ended and we would return to our classrooms.

During the time I was at Woods Hole School, we had a safety patrol program. We each had a white shoulder and waist strap assembly (shown on school class photo.) Each member had a metal badge. I was a lieutenant, so I had a blue badge. I think the captain had a red one. My *post* was at the top of the stairs on the second floor. I remember that there was a post somewhere on the playground and another about a quarter mile away at the corner of School and Millfield Streets.

Back in those days, we brought our lunches to school in a bag or, more frequently, in a metal lunch box. I had a Superman lunchbox. One day my friend "N" brought a surprise to school in her lunchbox. Her dad was a scientist at a lab down town and they were using white mice for experiments. "N" loved all kinds of animals and she decided that she would bring a couple of the mice to school in her lunchbox. She was anxious to show her teacher and the other kids the little white mice.

Well, somehow the mice got out of her lunchbox and started running around the classroom. Needless to say, this did not go well. There is more to write about those early school days, but this is all that I can recollect clearly after all these years.

Pendergast Family Photo

Me – 2nd row down, sixth from the left

Me – top row, 6th from the left

THE CHILDREN'S SCHOOL OF SCIENCE

During the summer months, the Woods Hole School is the site of The Children's School of Science (CSS). The CSS is an internationally recognized summer learning experience. It was founded in 1908 and celebrated its centennial in 2008. The CSS offers a unique, hands-on approach to scientific learning for students ranging in age from seven to sixteen. Many interesting courses are offered that would not be available in a lot of public school curriculums. Many of the courses include field trips to explore the Cape Cod environment. Following is an article that some of you may find very interesting. Perhaps you may know of a young student who would be interested in attending this fine learning program.

*****

The Children's School of Science encourages and develops in children a love and appreciation of science. Inquiry, direct observation, and understanding of nature guide our instructional philosophy. Frequent field trips and hands-on classroom study give students the opportunity to explore nature, become adept at observation, and discover the rules that govern natural processes. The world-famous scientific community of Woods Hole offers additional opportunities to learn about research in different fields. The unusual complexity of the waters, geology, and biology of the greater Falmouth area provides a uniquely well suited "live" learning environment. Courses are organized into three-week (A session runs from July 1 to July 19, and B session from July 22 to August 8) and six-week sessions (AB runs from July 1 to August 8.) Introduction to Photography, Comparative Habitats, and Black and White Film Photography can be taken as a four-week class (designated A+) or as a six-week class (AB). Classes meet daily Monday through Friday for ninety minutes. Attendance at every class is expected. Courses are organized according to students' interests and age appropriate study. Children may enroll in the youngest class if they reach the age of 7 years by the time they start Science School, and have finished first grade. Students under 10 are discouraged from enrolling in more than one class per session. A $35 fee is due at the time of registration. **Tuition for one six-week course is $450, one four-week course is $345 (listed as A+), and tuition for each three-week course is $260.** It is the policy of the Children's School of Science that tuition is non-refundable.

Scholarships: Partial scholarships are available to those truly in need. Please send a written request for financial aid to general@childrensschoolofscience.org.

CSS is run by volunteers. All parents are asked to volunteer whenever possible; however, at a minimum, all parents of enrolled children are required to provide transportation for at least one field trip, or to work at the CSS front desk for two class periods, per three week period enrolled. **Please note that additional children may not accompany you on your volunteer duty.**

VANDALS STRIKE

Imagine if you will a beach party on Cape Cod. A group of about twenty teenagers is sitting in a loose circle around a waning fire. It is now the end of August. After a spectacular sunset, it has become full dark. In the distance, the mournful sound of a foghorn can be heard. Someone is gently strumming "Michael Row the Boat Ashore" on his guitar. A few kids are singing along softly. There is the occasional hiss as a damp remnant of driftwood catches in the fire. The odor of smoke hangs in the night air. Just now, there is the familiar *pop* of a can of a *Colt 45* being opened.

The year is 1962, and another memorable summer has come to a close in Woods Hole. The mood is somewhat bittersweet tonight. Some summer romances are ending. Promises to write are made. A few tears are shed. One couple takes their blanket and walks hand-in-hand down the beach. Most of these young people winter out of state. They have come down for the summer with their families so that their parent(s) can do research at the Marine Biological Laboratory (MBL.) Some kids are here because their folks have rented a cottage for a month or two during the summer. The remaining segment are local kids such as myself, who live here year round. Most of this eclectic group will be back in high school in a few weeks, others starting college.

I can't recall exactly how the following incident came about. All I can remember is that it was quite late in the evening when the party broke up. Someone poured saltwater on the fire to

16

make sure it was out. Almost everybody left for home – some in cars, some on bikes, others walking. It had been a great evening.

However, there were still five of us left gathered there, three boys and two girls. I can only remember the name of one of the girls (P) who was a "year-rounder." Someone suggested the idea of running the two miles out to Penzance Point and back just for the fun of it. I don't remember who thought of it or why we would even *want* to do it at that hour. I guess the fact that it was a private peninsula, closed off to the public in the daytime, was the main attraction.

Penzance Point is a truly gorgeous place surrounded on three sides by water. It is basically a narrow arm reaching out into the ocean, shaped somewhat like a miniature Cape Cod. Back in 1863, it was the site of the Pacific Guano Company. This was a very successful operation for twenty-five years. The plant used guano (bird excrement) imported from South America. This guano was mixed with other ingredients to make fertilizer. This fertilizer was used by all the local farmers and those not so local. The plant closed in 1879.

Over the course of time, very wealthy people bought up acres of land out on the point and built large mansions overlooking the ocean. Some of the notable owners included the Nobel Prize winning scientist Dr. Albert Szent-Gyorgyi, who isolated Vitamin C; the Paul Mellon banking family; the owners of the Weyerhaeuser "Timber" Lumber Company; and, the Murray Crane family, who owned the Crane Currency Company in Dalton, Massachusetts, that made the paper used for printing the United States currency.

Many of these estates had guest houses, boat houses, and private docks to secure the owners' yachts. Almost all of these estates were only occupied during the summer months. The road to the point was blocked off with a security agent stationed at the entrance. If he didn't recognize you as a resident, he would stop your car, ask who you were visiting, and then call the host's house to see if you were expected. This cop was stationed there all day. However, at night there was no cop at the booth.

Therefore, at night anyone could drive out there. Weird type of security system! But that's how it was back in 1962.

The five of us ran right past the empty security booth. We continued running passing many driveways that led to the private homes. Finally we ended up at a driveway where we were confronted by three signs. The first announced the owner's name. Next to it were two signs saying "**Private Property**" and "**KEEP OUT**." We could see the main house and a boat house in the distance. There were some lights on in the main house, but the boat house was dark. There was a private dock jutting out into Great Harbor. Several boats were tied up the dock. We ran across the lawn, through the boathouse, and out onto the dock, somewhat out of breath.

*****

There were several boats tied up out there. The only two boats I remember were a 14-foot Boston Whaler and a larger fishing boat. Someone (can't remember who) suggested we see if it would start. He crawled up onto the seat and began tinkering around with the ignition. Bingo! The engine started. Someone untied the mooring line, and within a few minutes we were all heading out into the harbor.

What happened next is not clear in my memory. It was a very dark night with only some dim light from the moon and the soft glow from a few distant yachts. We rode around for twenty minutes or so. At some point, we scraped against something in the water. I think it may have been a buoy. Anyway, there was a loud grating sound and reality suddenly kicked in. We decided we'd better return the boat and get out of there ASAP. As we approached the dock, it was hard for us to see exactly where the boat had been tied up and where the mooring line was. Somehow the guy piloting the boat got rattled and revved the motor instead of idling it. Wham! Bang! We crashed into the dock. Holy Crap! We're screwed! Someone grabbed a piece of line off the dock and hastily tied the boat up.

When we hit the dock, some of us fell into the water. The water was about four feet deep, and we were soaked head to toe. Mass confusion. We crawled up onto the dock and ran away as fast as we could across the long front lawn. We sped down the driveway without looking back. Once on the tarred road, we all strained to keep up the pace to get off the point and back to the town. I remember that I was running beside P. Funny what I do remember…I had on a dark green turtleneck sweater…my favorite sweater. As we ran along, I said to P: "Oh, damn it. My favorite sweater is ruined."

She replied: "Don't worry. I'll buy you another sweater."

That, by the way, never happened.

Eventually we all got back to the center of town and split off, heading to our individual houses. I silently climbed upstairs to my bedroom, pulled off my wet clothes, threw them on the floor, and jumped into bed. I was totally exhauster and glad to be home.

AFTERMATH

I remember one day I was sitting in my mother's real estate office when she asked me to go down to the drugstore and get me a copy of the paper.

I went down the street, paid my 10¢, and picked up a copy

of the *Falmouth Enterprise*. In the middle of the front page was an article in bold print: **Boat Is Stolen From Penzance Point Dock**. There was a $50 reward offered for information leading to the identity of the culprits.

SWIMMING CLASSES have begun at the public beaches, and here Mike W. Costello, lifeguard at Megansett, is shown with some of his large class of intermediate swimmers.

Boat Is Stolen From Penzance Point Dock

Someone apparently drove out onto Penzance Point Friday night or early Saturday, untied deck and used it on some nocturnal errand, returning it damaged to the dock before daylight.

The boat's owners could not tell from their fuel gauge how far the boat might have been driven. Back with prop badly scraped, propellor knicked, gunwhales gouged and nose dented. She was tied up again with an old piece of line. Found on her deck was a part of a broken cleat of oak, splashed with white paint and

the turn-around in front of the house, stop and then drive away with lights out.

"Oh, man, I don't believe this. What's next?"

I remember giving the paper to my mother and turning to look out the window.

"Oh my, Phillip, what is this world coming to?"

"Ummmm…I don't know, Mom."

In the weeks following this mindless escapade, I was relieved that we hadn't been caught. Woods Hole, being a very small village (permanent population of 700 people), there was a fair amount of gossip about the article in the local paper. People wanted to know who the vandals were and became more vigilant. Would they strike again? Car keys were no longer left in ignitions. Many people started to lock their doors for the first time. Miraculously, we had not been caught on the estate. Back then there were no motion sensors or security cameras. Also, there were no guard dogs about. We would have never gotten away with that kind of trespassing today. Also, apparently no one saw us running down that long, winding road back to the center of town. Moreover, not one of the culprits had loose lips. Amazing!

CONTRITION

However, being a devout, eighteen-year old Irish Catholic, I was filled with remorse and guilt. The fact that I was an altar boy made it all the worse. ERGO: I felt compelled to confess this criminal act. Therefore, after much discussion with myself…off to confession I went.

I remember well walking into our little village church one Saturday afternoon. Since it was so bright and sunny outside, it made the interior of the church seem even darker than it was.

There was the soft glow of some offertory candles in little red jars on the tray next to the communion rail, and the faint smell of incense hung in the air. The confessional (the sweat box) was off in the right corner. I took a deep breath, squared my shoulders, and walked slowly toward the box. I dreaded what was to come. I knelt down on the padded kneeler with sweating hands. Once that screen slid open there was no turning back. The priest pulled back the curtain. "Bless me, Father, for I have sinned, and it's been a long time since my last confession."

A voice said, "Go on."

I went through my normal, boring litany of misdeeds. Then it was *Showtime.* "Well, me and my friends stole a boat...and..... and...We got in an accident."

"Go on."

"Well...er...we went out to Penzance Point and borrowed a boat...and.... and.... we..."

"You went out to Penzance Point and *stole* a boat?"

"Yes, Father."

SILENCE.

"So we went out on the dock and there was a large boat and several small boats tied up...So we...uh...untied the larger boat and somehow started it up...and...er...um....rode around Great Harbor for a bit...and...um...."

"You just took it for a joy ride?"

"Yes, Father."

"Then what happened?"

"Well...er...it was really dark and there was really no light...except from the moon...and as we raced back to the estate looking for the dock, we had trouble finding the exact spot we took the boat from."

"Go on."

"My buddy who was steering the boat suddenly panicked……and crashed into their dock...and..."

"You crashed into their dock? Was the boat damaged?"

"A little, but it was an accident."

There was a long silence and then he said, "Well, let's see here. These people own a big estate on Penzance Point? They have a private dock with a big boat and smaller boats tied up out there?"

"Yes, Father."

"Hmmmmmm…well, I'm sure they must have had plenty of insurance, so I'm sure it was all covered."

"Oh, yes. I'm sure it was, Father."

"All right, then say three Our Fathers and three Hail Mary's. Now make a good Act of Contrition."

"Oh, my God, I am heartily sorry for having offended thee and I detest all my sins………"

"Good. Go in peace." The curtain and screen closed then opened again. "Oh, by the way, Phil, don't forget you're on the schedule to serve at the 9 o'clock Mass tomorrow morning."

"Yes, Father."

Well, so much for an anonymous confession.

*****

Author's Note: According to the Bureau of Labor Statistics Consumer Price Index Inflation Calculator, in today's currency, that $50 reward would have been a $424.79. That seems like a small reward offered by a multi-millionaire.

I don't know anything about the car mentioned in the paper. Curious tourists sometimes wandered out there at night.

ST. JOSEPH CHURCH

St. Joseph Church is located at 33 Millfield Street in Woods Hole. It is the second oldest existing church on Cape Cod. It was built and dedicated in 1882. The land was donated by Joseph Story Fay. The rectory, next door, was built in 1888. Due to a shortage of priests, the church is now only open from Memorial Day until Labor Day. Sunday Masses are at 9:30AM.

Back when I grew up, St. Joseph was a very active parish and the church was open year round. I was an altar boy at that church from age 10 – 15. I have many happy memories of this cozy little village church. I remember that during the summer months there was a wonderful little choir (6 – 8 people) that sang in a room off to the right of the altar. Mrs. West, a lady from West Falmouth, drove down to lead the choir.

As I recall, when I first moved to Woods Hole at the age of seven, Father Stapleton was the parish priest. He was followed by many fine priests over the years.

Of all the priests I ever met there, Father Bean was my all-time favorite. He spent many summers as an assistant priest during the 1950s. During the academic year, he taught English literature at Holy Cross College. I believe he was of the Jesuit order. When I met him, he was an older gentleman. He was a witty and very interesting man who had a great love of people, from little kids to senior citizens.

Here are some of my recollections of him:

He used to say to me that we were related.

"Your mother's name is Macbeth, right?

"Yes, Father."

"Well, it goes like this: The Macbeths branched off into the Macbeaths. Then the Macbeaths branched off into the Macbeans. Then the Macbeans branched off into the Beans. So, you see, we are related."

"Ah, I see what you mean, Father."

I remember Father Bean had a glass eye. So it sometimes appeared that he was looking off to the right. As noted, Father Bean was extremely well loved by all the parishioners. Therefore he was frequently invited to dinner by many different folks. He had a dry, subtle sense of humor. One time he went to dinner at a neighbor's home across the street. These folks had eight children, one of which was a little boy, blind in one eye, who always wore a black eye patch. Father Bean told the boy that he too had lost an eye years ago. He then popped out his glass eye onto the table. Then he just picked it up and popped it back in again. I wish I had been there to witness the event.

Father Bean went for many strolls around the village. Many times he invited me to accompany him. Once he even took me over to Martha's Vineyard on a day trip.

Father Bean loved sports. He went to lots of Little League games at the ballpark located right behind the church. He very often gave a brand new ball to the all-star player of the day.

On hot summer days, he would walk around the corner to Stoney Beach. He would sit off to the side on the private beach side of the jetty.

Father Bean was well known by all the folks at the beach, especially the younger kids. One reason for sure was because when the ice cream man came, Father would toss a handful of quarters out onto the sand. Whoever found one had enough money to get an ice cream cone. Those were such wonderful days and I often reflect back on them.

Life was so much simpler and kinder then. I really miss that fine priest.

St. Joseph
Church

Altar Boys 1952
From left to right
Peter Russell,
Phil Pendergast,
Father Unsworth,
Roger Cardoza,
Jimmy Reilly

(taken from the Pendergast family photos)

THE CAP'N KIDD

Photo credit: Ray Burke

The Cap'n Kidd is a well-known bar / restaurant located at 77 Water Street, right in the center of Woods Hole. The rear deck overhangs *Eel Pond*. It was built about 1849 and operated as an ice cream parlor in 1918. In 1930 the building became a restaurant (actually more of a local watering hole) and since 1936 The Cap'n Kidd has become a local landmark. The original Kidd was much more rustic than it now is. The original chairs were nail kegs with leather tops nailed on. The round tables, with oilskin covers, were set upon huge barrels. The big pirate mural painted by Joe Moran in 1939 is still there. The mahogany bar was carved around 1865 and moved to the Kidd from an old hotel in Lowell, Mass. which was being razed around seventy years ago. The beautiful white marble armrest runs the length of the bar for approximately fifty feet. This historic bar may be the longest bar on the Cape. I remember that there used to be Chianti bottles with wicker around the bottom placed on each table. I remember the different colored candles placed in each bottle, and the wax ran down the sides in an array of colors.

The Cap'n Kidd has changed ownership many times over the years. The place was sold to the Augusta family in 1946. Leonie (Augusta) Charles and her son, Jack Cauley, ran the place starting at that time. I remember that Leonie Charles had curly red hair. Bill Crowley bought the place in 1970, and the family still owns the place today.

The Cap'n Kidd is sometimes referred to as a *Pirate* bar. It is said that pirates hung out in Tarpoulin Cove back in the day and that Captain Kidd left buried treasure somewhere in that area, still waiting to be discovered. There was even a rumor that Captain Kidd himself visited the place at one point. Unfortunately that would have been impossible since he was hanged in London, England in 1711.

There are, however, some very interesting events that have occurred at the Kidd over the years, such as the incident when a guy drove his Harley into the Kidd along the bar and out to the back deck. He had a beer and a meal and then rode back out. The staff seemed to accept this.

Then there was the time that one of the regulars (a well-liked gentle giant of a man) got shut off by the bartender.

This customer got offended and left in a huff. He came back shortly afterwards with a chain saw and cut off the front door. No one bothered him. Remorseful, he returned the next day and replaced the door. All was forgiven.

I have a couple of friends who used to dive off the rear deck and swim across Eel Pond to their house on Millfield Street.

At that time there was a piano up against the wall as you entered the Kidd. Sometimes my friends would roll the piano out to the street, play it a bit and then roll it back in again. Other times they would drop M-85s through the grids in the old drawbridge that was out front. They would wait until a group of tourists were getting ready to cross the bridge, then drop the bombs into the water and run off. As the tourists were crossing, the bombs exploded underwater and shot large sprays up through the open grids in the bridge. This trick always got results.

Recently an old Woods Hole friend called me to relay the following account that he had just remembered.

Back in the late 1960s on a September night, my friend and his buddy went to the Kidd for a beer. For some reason it was closed. Therefore they went over to the Leeside where they consumed quite a few beers and were feeling no pain. They decided to take a boat out along the Elizabeth Islands to raid some lobster pots. They hit the mother-load and got about 100 lobsters. They brought their load back to my friends' house in Woods Hole. They spread the lobsters out in the back yard and covered them with a tarp. It was late at night by then, and they went to bed.

The next morning, my friend was awakened by his father. His

dad was not pleased with all the lobsters crawling around his back yard. They collected all the lobsters and put them in huge buckets, covered them, and put them in the water. That night my friend and his buddy went back to the Leeside around nine o'clock or so. They got a bunch of their friends (about twenty local folks) and suggested going to the Kidd to have a lobster bake. The Kidd was still closed for some reason, however my friend had a key. They cooked up the lobsters in the kitchen and had a great feast.

The group finally left about midnight and locked the place up. Very early the next morning, my friend and his buddy went to the Kidd to clean the place up before the staff came in to open for business. When they opened the front door and walked in, the very first thing they saw was a pair of legs dangling over the bar. Whoever it was had been up in the attic and had fallen halfway through the ceiling. The legs were not moving. My friend climbed up into the attic and found a guy who they knew passed out cold. They dragged him out of the attic and sobered him up fast. Then they proceeded to clean up the kitchen and restaurant as quickly as they could. They locked up the place with the key and cleared out. Miraculously, my friend and his buddy were never caught. I wonder what the owner thought when he discovered the large hole over the bar. All in all, this quaint watering hole has a colorful history. If those old walls could talk, they would have a lot of tales to tell.

In 1973, some of the bartenders, organized by Tommy Leonard, decided to race from the Kidd to the Brothers Four in Falmouth Heights…a distance of 7.2 miles. This is a scenic route passing Nobska Light and continuing along the Shining

Sea bike path. On Wednesday, August 5th, 1973, the group of runners had grown to about 92 people. This was the start of the now-famous annual Falmouth Road Race. David Duba, a college student from Michigan, became the first official winner of the race. Johnny Kelly (a two-time Boston Marathon winner) ran the race at the age of sixty-five. He is only one of many famous entrants.

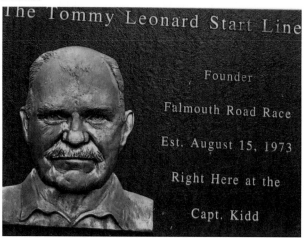

The Tommy Leonard Start Line

Founder

Falmouth Road Race

Est. August 15, 1973

Right Here at the

Capt. Kidd

Tommy Leonard
Photo credit: Claudia Pendergast Dion

The number of runners has grown dramatically and the race is now an international event. In 2020, more than 11,000 souls squeezed into tiny Woods Hole to run in this event. About 75,000 spectators gathered to watch the race from the start at the Kidd to the finish line at Falmouth Heights. Today there is a plaque in front of the Kidd honoring Tommy Leonard.

For almost a century many scientists, including Nobel Prize winners, students and countless tourists have enjoyed their drinks at the historic bar. The Kidd has also been the setting of some feature films.

NABBED IN A RAID

It was a quiet Friday evening at the Cap'n Kidd in Woods Hole center. My college roommate, Bob, and I were sitting in our booth enjoying our second Colt 45. Bob had just come down to the Cape to stay with us as he frequently did.

I had just turned twenty-one and could now drink legally. Bob, however, was still twenty. Before we left my house, my then girlfriend and future wife, Gail, had kindly loaned Bob her ID. Back in those days, no photo was featured or required on an ID. Her card merely stated her name, Gail F. Burke, height, hair and eye color, and date of birth. We figured the chances of Bob having to produce an ID were fairly slim. Back then, the Kidd was fairly relaxed about checking IDs. However, we did have to admit that neither of us had heard of any man named "Gail."

At any rate, Bob and I were laughing and reminiscing about some college adventures that we had shared. We were just about to order

On the way to The Kidd –
Bob Thaler and Phil Pendergast

another round when suddenly the room went very quiet. From each of the two entrance doors a man with a suit strolled in. Everybody put their drinks down and watched as the men approached each table. GREAT! It was an ABC (Alcohol Beverage Commission) raid. Not very common down there.

Bob said: "Crap, Phil! It's a raid!"

I said: "That's okay, Bob. I'm 21."

"You are moron, but I'm not."

"Oh, just give them Gail's ID and try to look pretty."

"Oh, that's so funny!"

We both sat there in silence looking out the window next to our booth. Eventually, one of the ABC men arrived and asked for our IDs. I handed him mine. He scanned it and handed it right back without saying anything. Bob handed Gail's ID over to the man. The guy looked at the card for a long time. He smiled and said to Bob: "So, you're Gail Burke?"

Bob looked down and quietly replied: "Yes, sir."

"Hmmmmm. Really? You don't look like a Gail Burke to me. But………. since you have enough nerve to pull this off, I will let you go this time. However, *Gail*, I don't ever want to see you in here again. Do you understand?"

"Yes, sir."

The man turned away and headed to the next table. Bob and I just sat there stunned. We both let out a sigh of relief and took a large gulp of our beers.

P.S. Bob never did use that ID again.

THE BREAKWATER HOTEL

The Breakwater Hotel was built sometime in the 1860s. It was originally erected as a structure to house workers for the Pacific Guano Factory located on what is now Penzance Point.

The guano factory went bankrupt in 1889. Horace Crowley bought it and moved it to its present sit on Bar Neck Road. He made sure that it faced Great Harbor, right across the street.

It became a hotel in the 1890s. The place was purchased in 1900 by Maria Bowman. Back in 1924, Miss Heloise Redfield became the manager. In 1940, Miss Redfield bought the hotel from a Mr. and Mrs. Robert Baker. She ran the hotel from 1940 to 1960.

One summer, when I was sixteen years old, I obtained my first real summer job as a waiter at the Breakwater Hotel. I remember walking up the front steps across the front porch and into the foyer. As I recall, Miss Redfield had her office on the right as you entered the foyer. She was a tall, thin lady with short grey hair and wore glasses. What I remember the most was that she loved her cats. She had some in her office and a few that wandered the hallways. Surprisingly, the guests didn't seem to mind them at all. The staff would sometimes joke about all the cats loitering around.

Miss Redfield hired young students for the summer as

maids, waitresses, waiters, and groundskeepers, etc. She even had a couple of detached bungalows out back where the help who did not live on the Cape could stay. The staff were all older than I and already in college. Even though they were older, they often included me in their leisure activities. I remember that I once attended one of their parties in a vacant summer house.

Back in the day, the Breakwater Hotel was really quite grand. It was the only hotel in Woods Hole. The nearest hotel was the Cape Coder Hotel in Sippewissett, which was torn down many years ago.

Over the years, many notable people stayed at the Breakwater. I wish I had a copy of an old guest register listing who these folks were. Very often the same people would return every summer and requested the same room and table. When I worked there one older lady always wanted to be seated at *her* table all the time. The staff was always informed by Miss Redfield of her guest's preferences. A funny thing I do remember is that the waitstaff was told to place a sugar bowl over any hole in a tablecloth...only one sugar bowl per tablecloth!

By the time I arrived on the scene, this once grand hotel was worn, tired and in need of major renovations. Miss Redfield did her best, but it was a huge place to keep up, both inside and out. I remember that there was an antique dumbwaiter system operated by rope and pulleys. The meals were prepared in a downstairs kitchen and hoisted up to the main floor dining room. I recall that there were covers over the plates to keep them hot.

As a waiter, I was supposed to place the meals on a large, pewter serving tray. I never got any specific training for this job, and I must confess I was not a good waiter. I never really got the hang of how to properly bus tables. I can't remember how I messed up. However, to be honest, you probably wouldn't have wanted me to wait on you. So, it is safe to say that I was the second dumb-waiter at that hotel.

Eventually, Miss Redfield had to let me go. I certainly didn't blame her. I did stay in touch via letters with a few of the waitstaff for a few years.

Sometime in the early 1960s, the Marine Biological Laboratory (MBL) bought the place. Unfortunately, this majestic hotel was raised shortly afterwards for possible expansion of the MBL. Sadly, this site remains empty and serves as another parking lot. Thus another Woods Hole landmark has disappeared

This concludes the story of my first summer job and my abbreviated experience at the famous Breakwater Hotel.

*****

Postscript: Fortunately for me I got a great summer job at the MBL supply department where I worked for five consecutive years.

Postcard photo

BREAKWATER HOTEL, WOODS HOLE, CAPE COD, MASS.

Phillip L. Pendergast

THE SQUID RUN

During the summer vacation months, from the time I was sixteen to twenty years old, I worked at the supply department at MBL, where samples of marine life were collected alive and then taken directly to be put in tanks of oxygenated salt water. From the supply department, these specimens were personally and carefully delivered to the various labs for research and experiments. Some of the items that I delivered from the supply department were dogfish, starfish, baby horseshoe crabs, arbacia (sea urchins), sponges, scup, goosefish, and different kinds of crabs.

Without any question, the most sought after and expensive specimens were squid. In fact a special fishing boat was chartered just to go out and collect squid. Squid were very popular because they had many parts that were used for research such as the eyes, the axon (the large dorsal nerve), and even the black ink they secreted to protect themselves if threatened or attacked. This ink was powerful and would temporarily blind or even kill their enemies.

I remember one summer when there was even talk of using the ink for ingredients in the manufacturing of hair dyes.

Every summer, a large group of scientists would come to live in Woods Hole expressly to do research on squid. A lot of this work was done on the axon. Therefore, the bigger the squid the better. Often times, scientists would come to the supply department to complain that they received smaller squid than the scientist in the adjacent lab. If I recollect correctly, I heard that two rival scientists even got into a fist fight over squid. As you can see, the scientists took their squid very seriously, and this had nothing to do with squid being used as a popular source of bait.

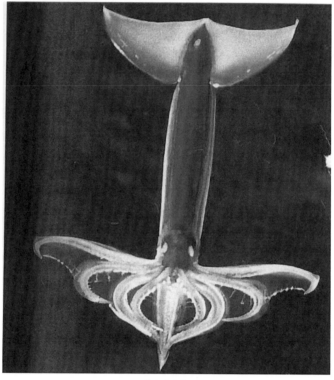

*****

One Saturday morning, my co-worker Tracy and I were in charge of the "squid run." We had to roll a big, heavy steel-lined container filled with fresh salt water all the way out to the dock to await the boat with the squid. This big container looked like a large coffin on wheels. When the boat finally arrived, our job was to carefully deposit the squid into this coffin of water. It was time consuming because each squid had to be deposited slowly, tail first, or else they would panic and ink. If one squid inked, then all the others would. Then our precious cargo would consist of a bunch of dead squid which were useless to the waiting scientists. All Tracy and I had to do now was to carefully deliver the squid to the various labs across the street and place them tail down into each tank. We had a squid list with about twenty names on it similar to this:

Lab #138 Dr. Lowengard 5 Squid

Lab #241 Dr. Hyashi 6 Squid

Lab #302 Dr. Lansing 4 Squid

Finally, the boat arrived and Tracy and I filled the portable tank and took off to deliver our precious cargo.

Tracy was in a hurry to get the "squid run" done as quickly as possible as he had a date waiting for him at 12:15. It was already 11:00AM, and we both got off for the weekend at 12:00 noon. The two of us pushed the heavy coffin across the main street and headed for the big red brick building where the labs were located. There was a service elevator, so we would have no trouble getting to all three levels. Since the tank was heavy with so many gallons of salt water, we took turns pushing it along. One time, when I was pushing it, I pushed a little too hard and the coffin accelerated due to the downward slope on the side street we were on.

It suddenly gained momentum and barreled down the street. Tracy and I ran after it, but it was moving too fast. It bombed down the street, hit the curb hard, and flipped over in the middle of the street. It was truly a horrible sight as the squid were flopping and inking inside the tank and all over the street. I can still see that overturned tank and the squid squirting out water and ink as they fell out of the tank and onto the blacktop.

Tracy and I ran to the tank and with great difficulty he and I turned it upright. We started just throwing the damned squid in as fast as we could. We must have tossed seventy or more squid back in the tank in a matter seconds. We didn't have time to put them in correctly. Besides the water was jet black from all that ink anyway. We got off the street as fast as possible and immediately ducked into the red brick building. This time we literally ran down the first-floor hallway. Usually we would announce "squid run" as we made our way on our rounds. This time we moved along very fast and said nothing.

We checked our list, opened the doors to the labs and dropped the squid into the tanks with the fresh, clean seawater. However, as soon as the squid landed in their new tanks, many of them started inking all over again. To make matters worse, the water in our delivery tank was inky black so we couldn't see the suckers (pun intended) and we had to blindly grope around for the squid. As a result, we were often grabbed by their tentacles and bitten by their beaks. Yup! Squid can bite. What a freakin' nightmare!

We used the freight elevator and managed to deliver to all three floors. The weirdest thing was that almost every lab was empty. Maybe the scientists took an early lunch. Who knows? There were only a few people working and those people were around the corner preoccupied with their slides and microscopes or whatever.

After we threw our last squid in its tank, Tracy and I ran back to the supply department. We rinsed out the portable coffin in time to check out just as the town horn sounded twelve noon.

What was most amazing about this episode was the fact that we got away with it without being caught. I was sure that we would be seen and our activities reported back to the supply department. Moreover, when our coffin spilled over onto that side street, it was completely free of people. And we were so lucky that our coffin didn't smash into a parked car or perhaps into someone crossing the street. Normally that street is very busy with people coming and going in and out of the various labs and adjacent buildings. Also, we didn't have to confront any scientists when we made our deliveries. They often stood in their doorways to make sure they were getting good-sized specimens.

I was sure that the following week Tracy and I would be reported by an unseen observer and either fired outright or at least be given a severe warning. Nothing ever happened. I'll never forget that Saturday morning over fifty years ago. I hope you'll reflect upon this the next time that you feast on your calamari.

Supply Department today – Pendergast Family Photo

A SEANCE & A OUIJA BOARD

Miss Florence Tinkham was a well-known local fixture in Woods Hole during the 1950s. She was born into a prominent family in Springfield, Massachusetts in 1885. Her father had been a very successful businessman. She was very well educated at Mount Holyoke College. She may have had a degree in marine biology, but I'm not sure. She moved to Woods Hole in 1907. From 1907 – 1930, she was a member of the MBL Corp.

She was a very private person who kept to herself. She lived in a large two-floor home that she had designed herself. Her property was located on the corner of Millfield Street and Albatross Street. Unfortunately, this lovely home has long since been torn down. Currently the Swope Building and a parking lot are located on that site.

Miss Tinkham also owned the lot across the street where she had a barn. She kept a goat tied up, and she had many geese. She kept the goat in order to have milk for her many cats. Miss Tinkham had an obsession with cats. She had scores of them. Some folks said she had twenty…other people said she had up to a hundred. At any rate, the cats were in her house and running all over the property. She was even referred to as "the cat lady" by some locals. She was very content being surrounded by her feline friends. She had names for some. As she acquired more and more cats, she gave up naming them.

I remember Miss Tinkham as always wearing black. She

wore long, black, draping-like dresses, even during the summer months. Over the years she became more and more reclusive. She enjoyed her privacy and didn't encourage visitors. She had a very large home that was screened off by a tall privet hedge out front. As I recall, the house was a faded silver-stained color with either dark green or black shutters. There was also a barn in the rear. Way back in the early '50s, the barn on the lot across the street burned down, leaving the large home and the barn in the rear. It was much reported that the firefighters found many shoe boxes with dead cats inside up in the loft. Come to think of it, this would have been a great setting for a Stephen King book or movie. A friend of mine who lived nearby had gone into the barn when he was a teen, before the fire. He said he saw some microscopes and lab equipment. He also saw some jars filled with what appeared to be formaldehyde and some cat remains in them. He is very honest and has an excellent memory, so I believe his account to be true.

Miss Tinkham suffered a stroke and died in 1960. She was seventy-five years old. For a time her large house remained vacant. Even though it was close to the sidewalk, it was hard to see the house because that hedge out front had grown so thick and high. This is now where my experience in Miss Tinkham's empty house begins.

*****

Miss Florence Louise Tinkham

1885 – 1960

*****

Photo source unknown

One day in the fall of 1960, some friends of mine and I thought it would be a good idea to see if we could get into the empty house and try a séance. We wanted to see if we could contact Miss Tinkham. I knew it was a weird, stupid idea. Nevertheless, we wanted to see if we could get inside the house. I believe it was October. The tourists were long gone and the village was quiet, with few folks walking around. Somehow, we did get inside the house. I think it was through the unlocked bulkhead. Not sure.

There were five of us as I recall: myself, a boy named C..., another boy F...and two girls whose names escape me. We sat around in a loose circle on the living room floor and held hands. I don't remember at all what we said. I think we each asked Miss Tinkham to send us a sign or something. After we had each tried and waited, nothing happened. I don't know if we were sad or glad. We all felt nervous, guilty, and uncomfortable being in the house.

We had also brought a Ouija board. Back in those days, using a Ouija board was a popular craze even though the board had been around since 1915. Anyway, we each tried to contact Miss Tinkham and several other deceased persons we knew. Alas. No results. No spirit provided any useful words or messages…just a few yeses and nos. We should have just quit then and gone home, but we didn't.

Instead, my friend C…. wanted to hypnotize F…. F…was from out of town and I don't even know why he was there that day. Anyway, I clearly remember F…'s face and his first and last name. C…had some kind of chain and he told F…to watch the chain swing back and forth in front of his face. Then F…was to close his eyes and keep them closed until C…snapped his fingers. C…told F…that when he opened his eyes he would not be able to talk. F…did as told. After a minute or so, C…snapped his fingers. F…opened his eyes. C…asked him to talk, but he couldn't. F…was wide eyed and he looked terrified. This lasted for what seemed a very long time, but it was probably only a couple of minutes. I can still see the fear in F…'s eyes. C…said "Okay, okay, close your eyes again and I'll snap my fingers and this time you can talk." C…snapped his fingers and F… could talk…and he did. He said he wasn't faking and he had been truly afraid.

47

At that point, everyone wanted to get out of there ASAP.

I don't understand what happened there, but something definitely did. We quickly left that old house the same way we got in. Nobody stole or disturbed anything. After that experience, I decided that I would not fool around with a séance, a Ouija board, or hypnosis ever again. I never did!

Side note:

Many years earlier, there had been a gristmill located on Millfield Street. Somehow, Miss Tinkham had obtained the millstone from the old mill and had it moved down the street to her property. She used it as a focal point in her garden. At some point after Miss Tinkham's death, the millstone was purchased by a Falmouth antique dealer. Apparently, Jaqueline Kennedy used to frequent the dealer when she was visiting the Cape. At any rate, Mrs. Kennedy bought the millstone from the dealer after JFK's death. She had it installed surrounding the eternal flame at JFK's gravesite at Arlington National Cemetery. If anyone is interested, they can still see the stone where it remains around the flame that burns in perpetuity.

I wonder what Miss Tinkham would think about the fact that millions of people had gazed upon the simple millstone that she had in her lovely garden.

HURRICANE CAROL

August 31, 1954

TRACKS, WIRE AND BUOYS plus a few sailboats made a melee of wreckage on the railroad tracks along Little harbor in Woods Hole. Looking east to Falmouth, the view was one of a pile of debris and warped and crushed railroad tracks.

Enterprise newspaper clipping from 1954

Our family was living on the Woods Hole Road directly across from Little Harbor when Hurricane Carol roared into town. I was ten years old. I remember the howling winds. The porch that ran across the front of our house was ripped right off. Our front door blew in, so my mother and I moved a large heavy bureau in front of it to keep it closed. I remember that the huge Coast Guard buoys were floating around like corks. Several buoys and some boats landed right on the railroad tracks that bordered Little Harbor. It was a fierce storm and it struck with a vengeance. Telephone lines

49

were down and the power went out. Carol was a category three hurricane with winds from 110 to 130 miles per hour. The storm surge varied from five to fifteen feet depending on the land elevation. The average surge in Woods Hole was over six feet in some low areas.

According to www.hurricanescience.org: "In total, 4,000 homes 2,500 cars and 3,000 boats were destroyed. There was a total of 68 deaths and about $400,000,000 in damages (1954 USD). Carol was the costliest natural disaster in US history until Hurricane Dianne surpassed it the following year."

Yacht washed on Penzance Point -
Lehy Family Photo

The little bungalow on Park Street, where we lived when we'd moved to Woods Hole in 1950, was totally flooded.

The house was located at the bottom of a small hill directly across from the beach. The water came rushing down the street, flooding everything in its path. I remember that there was a water mark on the living room wall indicating that the water level was about four feet high inside the house. The white Chevy Impala we had parked on the property was almost entirely under water. Needless to say, it was a total loss and we had to buy a new car. I don't remember why we had left one of our cars there since we had already moved up to the main road across from the harbor by that time. Fortunately, our summer tenant had just left and the property was vacant.

I remember seeing that one of the bath houses at Nobska Beach had blown across the street and into the pond. I also recall that there were some people rowing down the street in small row boats. Some kids were even swimming in the streets if I remember correctly. Also there were a few hardy souls still sitting at the bar at The Kidd as the water swirled around their feet. I think that *happy hour* started early and ran late that day.

I have a very vivid recollection of two beautiful yachts that had broken free of their moorings and washed up onto the road leading out to Penzance Point. Apparently they had been so badly damaged that they were beyond repair. Since they were so large and totally ruined, it was impractical to move them back into Great Harbor. Sadly it was determined that they should be burned on the road where they rested. I remember seeing the two huge fires when these beautiful yachts met their demise. This was indeed so very sad. This occurred sixty-seven years ago, but I can still picture it.

Boats washed up in front of the bell tower and Mary Garden –
Lehy Family Photo

Phillip L. Pendergast

LOST IN THE FOG

When I was thirteen years old, I got my first boat. It was a 12' wooden rowboat. I remember that I painted it light green and named it Katy for one of my sisters. I kept the boat at the little beach at the town landing, right by the Coast Guard station. I kept it pulled up onto the beach and tied up with a thick rope to a couple of cement blocks. Whenever I went out for a row, I brought my oars with me. I have many happy memories of rowing around Little Harbor.

The Katy I – Pendergast Family Photo

When I was about seventeen years old, my family bought a speed boat. It was a snappy red-and-white fiberglass craft called a Glasspar Marathon 1961 model. It was powered by a 35-horsepower Evinrude motor. It seated two people in the bow and two people in the stern. There was a steering wheel, gearshift device, and a windshield. It was, indeed, a very sporty boat, and it really moved! We had a mooring in Little

Harbor in front of the Lunn property. I kept my rowboat on the shore and just rowed out to the mooring whenever I wanted to take the Glasspar out. I tied up the rowboat at the mooring and just took off. It was a pretty simple procedure.

At this particular time, we lived in a house right across from Little Harbor and we could easily keep an eye on the Glasspar and our mooring.

The Katy II – Pendergast Family Photo

I remember trips to Tarpaulin Cove and over to Great Harbor. We would go water skiing behind the boat and we often went over to Falmouth Harbor Boat Sales to get petrol. Sometimes we would go around Great Harbor and Penzance Point and over to Stoney (MBL) Beach. We also occasionally went over to Martha's Vineyard for a day trip.

One summer evening in 1963, a friend of mine, his date, my girlfriend, and I decided to hop over to Martha's Vineyard to listen to the folk singer Tom Rush. He was appearing at the Moon-Cusser Coffee Shop in Oak Bluffs. The Moon-Cusser had just opened, and it was a very popular place to hear folk music at that time. James Taylor and the

Simon Sisters (Carly and Lucy) got their starts there when only teenagers. Many well-known singers also appeared there including Jose Feliciano, The Clancy Brothers, Doc Watson, Don McLean, Phil Ochs, and many others. Monday nights were "hootenanny nights" with open mics. The cover charge was only $1.50, and the place would hold up to 150 folks. Those really were *the days*.

This boat trip was pretty much a straight shot across Vineyard Sound, a distance of about 8–9 miles. We had done this before and, as I recall, it took about 30–45 minutes to get there.

We left Little Harbor about 6:30–7:00PM. I do remember it was still daylight. It was a beautiful, warm evening, and the sea was calm. We arrived at the island a little ahead of schedule. We found an opening at a local town dock and tied up the boat with two lines. We always seemed to easily find an empty slot to moor. No one had ever disturbed our boat while we were gone. I seriously doubt we would be able to do this today. When we got to the club, there were several guys playing guitars and singing. I think that they were some locals…not sure. Tom Rush came on next and sang for a while, took a break, and returned again. I don't remember much what he sang or the rest of our time at the club. I do remember that there was a good sized crowd there. Finally the show was over and it was time to return home.

We returned to the dock, untied the mooring lines, started up the motor, put on the running lights, and began our trip back to Little Harbor at Woods Hole. By now it was about

10:00PM and full dark. We had made this same trip several times before. However this time we had a serious problem. It quickly became apparent that a fog bank had rolled in. After we had gone a few miles, the fog got much worse. You could call it a "pea soup" fog. Even with our lights on, we couldn't see more than a few yards. It was a very scary experience. Now, all of a sudden, we were in a bad situation. As I remember, we did have a compass mounted on the dashboard. However, for whatever reason, it was of no practical use to us. We were completely disoriented by now, and we were not sure what direction we should actually go. We had no idea how far we actually were from Woods Hole. Of course, back in those days there were no cell phones. So, there we were: four teenagers out at sea at night in a thick fog with no phone. Also, during all this time, we were afraid that some larger boat may not see us and would crash into us. I remembered the tragedy when the Stockholm crashed into the Andrea Doria. The fog was a big factor in that incident. The Andrea Doria sank and fifty-seven people died. The lifeboats of the Andria Doria were retrieved and tied up at the Woods Hole Coast Guard Station across the street from our house

I wish I could remember how long we were floating around aimlessly in this dire situation. I do remember that eventually we saw some lights approaching us through the fog. We were all hoping that whoever it was saw our small boat. Thankfully it was the Coast Guard. Boy, were we relieved to see them! Apparently our parents had contacted the Coast Guard and reported us missing. I do not recall any of the details regarding our return to Woods Hole. I do know that the Coast Guard led us back to Little Harbor. It was convenient that this was where the Coast Guard station was located. They escorted us back to our mooring and waited as we secured the Glasspar and rowed the short distance to shore.

To this day, I feel bad about the pain and worry that this episode caused my mom and the other parents. We were very lucky to have had a safe return home. After that, we didn't take any more trips to the Vineyard at night.

DR. ALBERT SZENT-GYORGYI

Dr. Albert Szent-Gyorgyi was a world-famous Hungarian scientist who lived in Woods Hole year round. Of all the scientists in Woods Hole, he was probably the most well-known and beloved. He won the Nobel Prize for isolating Vitamin C. He had a home out on Penzance Point where he lived with his wife, Magda, who was also a scientist.

He searches for cure

Dr. Albert Szent-Gyorgyi of Woods Hole studies a chart he compiled recently in his 10-year search for a cure and prevention of cancer. (Staff Photo by Roger Murray)

Dr. Szent-Gyorgyi could often be seen riding his white motorbike from his home to his laboratory at the Marine Biological Laboratory (MBL) in Woods Hole. Everyone recognized him easily with his thick, white hair. He was affectionately known as *Prof.* by many of the local folks. During several summers when I was a teenager, I had the important job of washing test tubes in his lab. That was the closest I ever got to any scientific research.

The following article discusses Dr. Szent-Gyorgyi's work on searching for a cure for cancer. I thought that the reader would find the following article both interesting and informative.

Cape's Nobel winner fears lab closing

Scientist: Short funds

By ROGER MURRAY

WOODS HOLE — The Woods Hole scientist who won the Nobel Prize for chemistry nearly four decades ago for isolation of vitamin C is thoroughly convinced he is on the right track for a cancer cure — but he's frustrated by lack of funds.

Dr. Albert Szent-Gyorgyi, who heads the Institute for Muscle Research laboratory in the Marine B i o l o g i c a l Laboratory is fearful that his 10-year-old institute, which has devoted most of a decade to cancer research, may be curtailed or possibly closed if sufficient funds are not forthcoming to continue his studies.

"Since President Nixon took over, I have been unable to get one penny from the National Health Institute which funded me generously

before," Dr. Szent-Gyorgyi said. "I am carrying on with the greatest difficulty on private donations and a relatively small grant from the National Science Foundation, which is just sufficient to pay my rental at the MBL but does not cover research costs.

"Unfortunately, the American Cancer Society is more interested in the treatment of patients than in solving the cancer problem. I have written twice to the society asking them whether they would be interested enough in my work to make it worthwhile for me to apply. "Their answer was negative.

"Now we have a queer situation that Cape Cod has a most active cancer research group which is unable to work for lack of funds while Cape

Cod collects relatively great sums for cancer research and sends it all to Washington.

"I see definite possibilities not only to cure, but even to prevent cancer. This I owe to the fact that I think I have solved a few basic problems without which the solution of cancer work is hopeless.

"I think the disturbance in cancer is partly in the electronic level. My research indicates this disturbance in cancer is on an electronic level.

"If you cut yourself the wound heals, which means that the cells on the side of the wound multiply. If the wound is healed the cells stop growing. Thus, there is a regulatory mechanism to adjust growth to need. In cancer, this mechanism is out of order. We can control only

GERTRUDE WHITING

Gertrude Whiting was a world-famous artist who resided many summers in Woods Hole during the 1950s and 1960s. She was a distinguished landscape artist. However, she was especially acclaimed for her portrait paintings. Miss Whiting painted many famous people (ie: Dame Judith Anderson and Jimmy Durante) over her long career. Her portraits were very realistic, and she was often compared to the famous artist John Singer Sargent.

Miss Whiting had a studio in Woods Hole during the summer months. Her studio was located on Water Street, near the draw bridge in the center of the village where the Black Duck used to be. She lived in what is now known as the Bradley House, which is currently home of the Woods Hole Historical Museum.

During many summers, I took art lessons from Miss Whiting at her studio. She taught lessons in both oil and watercolor. She usually had a group of 6-8 in each class, ranging in age from fifteen to the seventies. She was a very encouraging teacher, and all her students loved her.

I still remember the smell of the canvases and oil paints.

Gertrude Whiting was a very proper, charming woman. She dressed very conservatively, usually in subdued colors of beige, brown, and black. I loved the sound of her voice; and, she had a very calming manner about her. Despite her name and notoriety, she led a very simple life. She would often remark to me: "Philip, most good artists end up in the poor house."

Gertrude Whiting often did portraits of some of the local folks…especially children. She once did an oil painting of me when I was about thirteen or fourteen years old. It appeared briefly in her front window. Unfortunately our family didn't have the money to buy it at that time. I often wondered what had happened to it. Often (as with many artists) she would paint another portrait over an older one. Maybe I was painted over. Fortunately, my mother was able to buy a watercolor of *Olde Main Road* – the road leading into Woods Hole's center. At one time we lived in the yellow house depicted in that painting. Right now, that painting – inserted below - is matted and framed and hanging in our living room.

Gertrude Whiting In Her New York Studio

Gertrude Whiting Painted, Formed Friendships Here

by Isabel Conklin

Gertrude Whiting, painter, of Old Lyme, Conn., died, unexpectedly, on March 31. She was 82.

A distinguished portrait painter and teacher of painting, Miss Whiting grew up in Cambridge and had her main formal art training in Boston, at the Boston Museum of Fine Arts school, and privately with Philip L. Hale and Martin Mower at the Fogg museum. She became drawn to portraiture, which continued to be her special professional life interest.

Going to New York city in the 1930s, she studied further, at the Arts Students League, and with W. Bridgeman and Wayman Adams. New York became her main place of work and her spiritual home for many years, most of the time from her studio apartment in the old Sherwood Studios on West 57th street.

In 1958 she left New York to take a position, which she held until 1970, as artist in residence at Chatham Hall, Va., where she taught classes in art, history and appreciation of studio work.

Retiring from Chatham Hall in 1970, she made her permanent home in Old Lyme and continued to work actively there in portrait painting.

She was a member of the Madison avenue church in New York city.

Gertrude Whiting was well known and had many friends in Woods Hole, where she painted and had studio classes in the summer in the 1950s, setting up a studio on Water street, near the drawbridge, in the location later, of the first Fishmonger restaurant and presently of the Black Duck. She made a home for herself, her paintings, her students and friends at what is now the Bradley House, home of the Woods Hole Historical Collection. She recognized the house, although it was then in disregard and disrepair, as a genuine and dignified old building, with a beautiful location and view; and rented it from the Woods Hole library, its owner, at a low price. She cleaned it up and redecorated it herself, with ruffled, unbleached muslin curtains, handmade, at every window, freshly painted and spattered floors, the big iron stove in the kitchen polished, and repapered walls glowing with her oil paintings. Many enjoyed her hospitality there.

Her two locations at Woods Hole survived several hurricanes. While there, Miss Whiting taught and painted a number of Woods Hole children. She attended the Church of the Messiah.

It was at her place in the Sherwood Studios during World War II that Miss Whiting, as her "war work," painted oil portrait sketches of Australian and New Zealand servicemen who were being put up, temporarily, at the Red Shield club of the Salvation Army.

Servicemen were invited to call for an appointment and come to the studio to "sit" to be painted. The portraits, on canvas, were later mailed to the young men's families back home. Miss Whiting corresponded with some of the men and their families for years. She was cited by the prime ministers of Australia and New Zealand for this work.

Very recently, she had correspondence with the present prime minister of New Zealand, who was one of her young subjects, in the war days.

Gertrude Whiting did portraits of many noted people — Margaret Sanger, Judith Anderson, Jimmy Durante, and the painters in New York, Takema Kajiwara, Louis Kronberg and Jack Connah, and Roger Tory Peterson. An Example of her work in Woods Hole is the portrait of Dr. E. G. Conklin in the library of the MBL.

Works by Miss Whiting are owned by the War Memorial in Australia, the Museum of the City of New York, the University of Georgia, Planned Parenthood of Tucson, Arizona, Union Carbide, Asahi company, Tokyo, Japan, and many private collections.

She is survived by a sister, Mrs. H. W. Rule, and a son, Clinton McKim of Boston, and three grandchildren.

MEMORIES OF MY LOVE BUG

I fell in love with her the first time I saw her in front of my house. The year was 1962, and I was eighteen years old. She was a real cutie with such a glowing, clean-scrubbed look. I just stood there a moment, my pulse pounding. She remained there, not moving an inch, just waiting for me. I could hardly wait to slide my hands over her nicely rounded rear end. This was all just too good to be true. I had a lot of plans for us starting that very evening.

The object of my lust was a brand new 1962 Volkswagen Beetle that my mom had bought for me. There was always some debate about her actual color. My girlfriend at the time described the color as "llama's breath green." I was kind of thinking "urine yellow." Either way, the color was unique.

Right then and there, she became my little *Love Bug*. Over the next several years, my *Love Bug* and I were to have many adventures. She was such fun to drive around. I loved the stick shift with the "H" format. There was a simple dial to control the heat. It was either on or off! There was an AM radio with two dials: one to select a station and another to control the volume. I remember that I usually had the volume turned up.

One of the features that I liked best about the car was that there was an "L" shaped tab on the floor that I could kick with my toe if the gauge read empty and I needed an extra gallon of gas to get to the nearest gas station. Gas was only twenty-five cents at that time and it only cost about $2.50 to fill the tank. The car averaged about 35 miles to the gallon, but I used that kick tab a lot, as I was always riding around short of cash. Hmmmmmmm......same problem today.

I had so many wonderful experiences with my little *Love Bug*. I drove it back and forth many times from my home in Woods Hole to UMASS Amherst where I attended college. I was fortunate to be able to rent space in a detached garage right off of campus. During winters it was a real break not having to brush off snow and de-ice the car. No matter the season or the weather, I was always on then go with my *Love Bug*.

My 1962 Love Bug – Pendergast Family Photo

One winter my roommate Bob and I drove to Marlboro, Vermont and back in one day. When we got to Vermont, it started to snow hard, and we ended up driving back to Amherst in a blizzard.

I also travelled to several other states including New Hampshire, Connecticut, New York, and Rhode Island. It is really hard to settle on my best adventures with the car, but the following episodes stand out most vividly in my mind.

*****

One Friday night, in October of 1963, Bob and I took our dates out for a fun evening at a local watering hole. This particular spot was very popular as the owners were very lax when it came to checking IDs. We were all under the drinking age of twenty-one. Two of us had fake IDs (no photos on driver's licenses back then.) Two of us had no IDs at all. We decided to drive up a mountainous road to a small pub called *The Pine Rest*. Yeah, I know, sounds like a nursing home. At any rate, we eventually made it to the summit of the mountain and settled in for a fun evening. The owners never did ID us. By now it was full dark and quite cold. But we were all warm and cozy inside, enjoying our mugs of beer and listening to our favorite songs on the juke box. It was one of those machines with buttons to press to select the 45 record you wanted to play. I think for twenty-five cents you got to play three selections. I recall that we always liked to hear *We'll Sing in the Sunshine* by Gale Garnett, *Satisfaction* by the Rolling Stones, and *Louie Louie* by the Kingsmen.

I remember that it was late in the evening when we all finally tumbled into the *Love Bug* for the ride home. Needless to say, at this point we were all feeling no pain. As we pulled out of the parking lot, we were struck by how poor the visibility was. There was a light drizzle, and fog had rolled in. Not the best night to be descending a mountain road that had no streetlights, especially in our condition.

I don't recall exactly how it happened, but at some point at the beginning of our descent, one of my knees hit the little tray under the steering wheel where the fuses were stored. The fuses fell out and rolled all over the floor and under the seats. All at once the lights went out and the horn wouldn't work. Instant panic hit along with a quick reality check. We could see nothing ahead of us and could barely see the edge of the road. If it hadn't been foggy, it wouldn't have been quite so bad.

One of the girls got hysterical and shouted out: "We're all gonna die!" I doubted that, but we surely did have a big *problema*. I drove along very slowly with my head out the window to see better. The others also had their heads out the windows to try to help. Since it was so late, only a few other cars passed us from the other direction. They honked their horns at us to let us know we had no lights.

I slowed down to barely a crawl and hugged what I hoped was the side of the road. Eventually, after a long and stressful ride, we got back to the campus. We could now see clearly from the streetlights, parking lot lights, and lights from the dorms. We dropped our dates off at their dorms. Once we got back to our dorm, we each took two aspirin and went right to bed. The next day, Bob and I collected the little fuses from off the floor and under the seats where several of them had rolled. We carefully installed them back into the little tray and snapped the tray back in place. All was good. Once more the *Love Bug* was ready for its next adventure.

*****

One Saturday morning in October of 1964, I decided that

it would be fun to drive to Manchester, Connecticut for the day to visit an old friend with whom I had gone to prep school. It had been a while since we had gotten together, and it was always fun when we met up. I called my friend Dick, and he said he was free and would be happy to see me again. We agreed to meet at his house in Manchester at two o'clock that day. I asked him if he minded if I brought a friend along to talk to during the long trip there and back. He said, "Sure, why not? I'll see you later this afternoon."

I immediately called my friend Kathy and asked if she wanted to go on a spur-of-the-moment ride to Connecticut. She said she had nothing planned, was bored, and would love to go on an adventure. Within the hour, I picked up Kathy at her dorm. She hopped into the beetle and were on our way. There was no GPS back in those days. However I did have a good map from the AAA that covered all of Massachusetts and most of Connecticut. It was a sunny fall morning, not a cloud in the sky. Perfect weather for a day trip.

After we had been driving for about an hour, I realized that we had accidently turned off the highway and that we were now driving into what appeared to be a quaint old New England town. I didn't catch the name as we exited the ramp. We drove through what I assumed was the town's center. We then turned down a side street. At the end of that street, we turned right onto another side street. After going a few blocks, we came upon a group of brick buildings. It looked to me like several abandoned factories of some kind. I didn't notice any signs. I turned into a driveway which led to a huge parking lot that abutted a few more brick buildings. The parking lot was empty and the whole place looked pretty dingy and forlorn. I pulled the VW to a stop at the far end of the parking lot. I knew we were really lost and had no idea where we were. Kathy took out our map and we were just starting to look at it when I had a sudden thought.

"Kathy, do you want a drink?"

"What are you talking about? It's only about noon time."

"I know, but my buddy gave me a half empty bottle of Bellows whisky that he got at a party. It's in the glove box and I have some plastic cups in there also."

"Oh, man, Phil! You're funny. Why not."

I opened the glove compartment, took out the pint of Bellows, and poured a few shots worth into the clear plastic cups. I put the bottle on the floor and set the cups into the two recessed slots on the inside cover of the glove compartment which was now open and functioning as a small tray.

"Ah, time for a quick nip of *Bellows*, my favorite whiskey."

"I was just reaching over to give Kathy her cup when she said, "Did you hear that noise?"

"No, why?"

"I dunno. I feel like somebody is out there. This place gives me the creeps."

At that precise moment, I looked in my rearview mirror and saw a black and white pulling up slowly behind us. No siren. No flashing blue lights. The cop car came to a quiet stop. Very quickly, I slammed the door to the glove compartment shut, throwing the two cups, whisky and all, right into the box. Then I kicked the pint of *Bellows* under my seat. The door to the cruiser opened and a state trooper very slowly strode up to my driver's window.

He said, "Do you know where you are?"

"Someplace in Connecticut."

"Good guess. You're in the rear parking lot of the Wethersfield State Prison."

"Oh, I didn't see any signs."

"The prison shut down last year. This is private property. You don't belong here. What are you even *doing* here anyway?"

"I'm on my way to visit my friend in Manchester. I took a wrong exit off the highway, so I pulled in here to check my map and rest a bit."

"Well, I guess you certainly are lost. You've got a ways to go yet before you get to Manchester. Listen up. When you exit this parking lot, turn left. Turn left again at the third set of lights. You will see several signs for Manchester. Just follow the signs to the expressway entrance. You can't miss them."

"Oh, thanks, officer."

He said, "No problem."

I said to Kathy, "Whew. That was close. Let's get out of here fast."

The trooper went back to his cruiser and sat down in the driver's seat. I think that he was writing something down, but I wasn't sure. For some reason, he had left his door wide open. I started my car up and shifted into reverse. I don't know how, but somehow, in my haste to get away, the rear fender of my car hit the edge of his car door, causing it to slam shut.

"Holy shit! I can't believe I did that!"

Kathy and I just stared at each other in shock.

"What the hell! You just hit my cruiser! Are you crazy?! Don't get out of your car. Stay right in your seat."

Kathy and I sat rigid in our seats, not moving an inch. The trooper got out of his car and checked his car door very carefully. Then he walked very slowly up to my driver's window.

"Look kid, you are *very very* lucky. There appears to be no damage. Now listen to me *very* carefully. Drive out of this parking lot and out of this town and never come back." He walked back to his cruiser, got in, and drove slowly away.

I waited about five minutes or so, hoping that he was not parked around the corner. I slowly exited the parking lot and pulled out onto the street. He was gone. I followed his directions and got back on the expressway with no trouble.

Kathy and I arrived safely in Manchester and met my friend as planned. We had a great visit. We drove back to UMass later that night.

I have not returned to the town of Wethersfield, Connecticut and never plan to.

*****

It is with a heavy heart that I write this last section. One Saturday night in November 1964, I went to a party at a friend's house in Woods Hole. I lived in Woods Hole, but my date that evening lived in Falmouth Heights, about a fifteen-minute ride away. I hopped into my *Love Bug* wearing my brand new white turtleneck cable-knit sweater. (Yes, I love sweaters.) I was in great spirits because my winter break from college was just starting.

It was a clear but cold night. Right away I turned on the dial to get some heat in the car. It was around 7:30 or so when I arrived at Candy's house. Candy met me at the door and we took off for the ride back to Woods Hole. When we arrived at the house, the party was in full swing. There were probably about twenty young people there. The only name I recall was Peter, who was hosting this get together.

I do remember that Peter's parents were away for a few days, so we had the place to ourselves. I recall that on the dining room table there was an assortment of about seven or eight bottles containing different kinds of liquor: Jack Daniels, Scotch, Vodka, Gin, etc. There were also cans of soda if needed. There was music blaring from a hi-fi somewhere, and everyone was having a grand old time. I wish I could remember more about the details of the party, but it was fifty-five years ago, and I just can't remember any particulars. I do recall that we were just about all under the legal drinking age of twenty-one, and almost everyone had sampled some of the different bottles that were available on the table.

Around midnight or so, I decided that I'd better get Candy back home. I remember getting back into the car and turning up the heat full blast. I turned on the AM radio and dialed up a station that specialized in the *Golden Oldies*. As we pulled out of the driveway, I saw that a light powdery snow was just starting to fall. I drove Candy home along the shore road and back to her house without incident. It had been a very pleasant evening conversing with friends, some of whom I hadn't seen in a while.

As I was driving down a long stretch of the deserted road leading back to the shore road, I observed that the newly fallen snow was starting to accumulate. For some reason that I do not understand, I decided that it would be fun to zig-zag back and forth across the road. Since it was late at night, there were no other cars on the road. After zigzagging across the road about five or six times, I went into a skid and slammed right into a telephone pole. The top of the pole broke off somehow and there were sparks shooting into the air and lots of loose wires hanging down. Even worse, the top of the pole was on fire. The whole left side of the car was bashed in and the passenger side window had disintegrated.

In addition, my horn was blaring loudly and I couldn't shut it off. Thank God I had gotten Candy home safely. I got out of the car and pulled the fender away from where it had jammed against the wheel.

I jumped back into my car and drove as quickly as I could down to the shore road. I just wanted to get out of there as fast as possible. It was driving me crazy that the horn was still beeping. After about ten minutes of driving along like this, I saw blue lights in my rearview mirror. The black and white pulled right up behind me with lights flashing back and forth.

Oh, man. Oh, man, I thought.

I remained in my banged up car with the damned horn still screaming. A cop strode over to the driver's window and stood there a minute, staring at me through the glass. I rolled my window down and looked up at him. I remember exactly what he said: "Do you realize that you just left the scene of the crime?"

"What crime?"

"That phone pole you hit back there is on fire."

"Oh."

"Give me your license and registration." He quickly scanned them. "Do not get out of the car. Stay right there. I can smell the alcohol on your breath.". (They didn't have a breathalyzer test back then. No matter. It was obvious I'd been drinking.) "You're not 21. Where'd you get the booze?"

"I'm not telling on my friends."

"Listen up…. If you don't tell me, you're going to be in a lot more trouble than you already are."

"Okay, I was at a party at a friend's house in Woods Hole and there were a bunch of bottles on the table. I don't know how they got there."

"Whose house was this party at?" I told him. "Where were the parents?"

"I don't know. They were away somewhere."

"All right, get out of the car and come with us. Get into the back seat."

I did as told and sat in the back of the cruiser. It was then I saw that there was a second cop sitting in the passenger's seat.

"All right, Phillip, where do you live in Woods Hole?"

"19 Nobska Road."

"Just sit tight. We're taking you home." As the cruiser

pulled away, I turned and looked out the window at my beloved *Love Bug* with one side bashed in and the horn still blaring. I knew the car was totaled. I felt just terrible.

AFTERMATH

Within a few minutes, we arrived at my house. One of the cops marched me to the back door and rang the bell. My mother was upset but handled it better than I would have. I felt so bad that I had let her down. I never did get any fine. However, I did lose my license for three months. As fate would have it, my accident occurred right in front of the house of a reporter for the *Cape Cod Standard Times*. This time, my name did make the paper. A few days later, a small article was buried on page three of the paper stating that there was a car accident Saturday night and that a phone pole was damaged and caught fire. The reporter was very gentle with his wording of the incident. It stated that *His light foreign car slid on the newly fallen snow*. There was no mention of any alcohol.

*****

Author's Note:

I almost didn't write this short story due to its sad ending. However, I decided to include it in *Woods Hole Daze* as a tribute to my little *Love Bug*…. the best car I ever owned. I wish so much that I had that 1962 Beetle sitting in my garage right now. I've often thought of buying an old 1962 Beetle, but it just wouldn't be the same. My *Love Bug* is long gone….. but it will live on in my memory forever.

RIP dear friend.

THE LOST CITY OF ATLANTIS

For over 2000 years, many people have been intrigued by the legend of the lost city of Atlantis. There has been much speculation as to whether or not it even existed. Was Atlantis really an advanced civilization buried for centuries beneath the sea? Why and how did it disappear? Was Atlantis real or simply a myth or legend, a fantastic imagining of the human mind? So much has been written about this "long lost" city that one can easily get baffled by all the unproven theories. Moreover, the search for this ancient city has picked up a lot of momentum in the 20th and 21st centuries.

There are a few things that we actually do know: The word *Atlantis* derives from the Greek and has been interpreted to mean the *Island of Atlas*. Plato first mentioned the concept of Atlantis in his work *Timaeus and Critias* which was written around 360BC. Some scholars think this story was simply written as an allegory pointing to the destruction of prideful mankind. However, many scholars think the Plato was alluding to the sudden, total destruction of a highly advanced metropolis. And so the controversy rages on to the present day. A majority of folks believe that Atlantis is just a tantalizing, fantastical legend. But there are many scientists, historians, and explorers who continue to believe that the remains of Atlantis are still buried at the bottom of the sea. Alas, who really knows?

One of the more popular theories is that the volcanic Greek island of Santorini (Thera), located in the Aegean Ocean is the site of this fabled lost city. In his fascinating book *Voyage to Atlantis*, Doctor James Mavor, Jr., from the Woods Hole Oceanographic Institution (WHOI) in Woods Hole, recounts his expedition in search of Atlantis on the WHOI vessel *Chain*. Doctor Mavor was a well-known oceanographic engineer and one of the designers of the famous two-person deep sea submersible *Alvin* that was instrumental in locating a missing H-bomb off the coast of Spain.

Doctor Mavor, in 1965, began researching the mystery of Atlantis. He went on to organize two expeditions to the Aegean Sea in search of this lost city. He believed that he had discovered the actual site on the volcanic island of Santorini.

During the autumn of 2005, my wife, Gail, my sister Kate, her boyfriend, and I had the experience of renting a villa on the edge of a sheer cliff on the beautiful island of Santorini. Over the years, I have been fortunate to have visited forty-two countries. I can honestly say that, in my opinion, the island of Santorini is the most gorgeous place I have ever seen. Words fail to adequately describe this magical island. Everywhere I turned to look was a photo-op. We stayed in Fira, in the town of Oia. Our villa was perched on the rim of the caldera overlooking the Aegean Sea which has long since filled in the volcano. This ancient volcano is said to have erupted in the largest seismic event ever recorded by man until that time. This catastrophe occurred around 1500BC and destroyed most of Santorini and obliterated the Minoan settlements. The view that we had as we sat out on our patio was spectacular. We also enjoyed the sunsets every night that Santorini is so famous for.

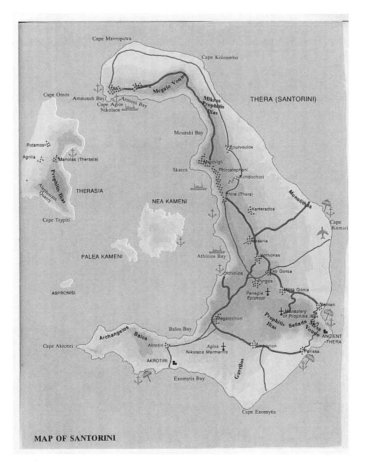

MAP OF SANTORINI

I have included this map of the island of Santorini and a photo of our view with the volcano and caldera in the distance. I hope that you found this background information interesting. Who knows? Perhaps you will decide to visit Santorini sometime in the future. It would be an exotic setting for a honeymoon and certainly well worth the time and money to travel there.

TRIBUTE TO MY DAD

RICHARD L. PENDERGAST
1913-2000

Although my dad did not live with us during our growing up years, he was still a very real presence in our lives. He lived on Beacon Hill in Boston and worked at the State House. My sister Kate and I would make frequent trips to Boston to visit him. My mother would put us on the train at the Depot Station in Woods Hole. My dad would be awaiting us at South Station in Boston. This system worked out very well. Also, we spent time with him during the important holidays. At this time I would like to share with you some thoughts about my dad. Many of these words are taken directly from my dad's writings. Some were spoken by me in the eulogy at the Mass and memorial service in 2000.

*****

My father was a true gentleman with a keen mind. He was an avid reader up until a few months before his death at the age of eighty-seven. In fact, he had just recently re-read James Hilton's Lost Horizon. *He had an excellent memory and could recall many events from books he had read many years before. I would like to read to you a portion of an article that my father had written only a few years ago and submitted to a magazine for publication.*

"FROM THE BEGINNING"

"I was lucky when I was a boy growing up. I was born in 1913 into a family with 2 girls and 2 boys and in 1918 my mother gave birth to another son. While battling the Spanish Flu, raging through the western world, she lost the battle to the flu, but the baby, Edward, made it. Unfortunately, he later died when his ship was sunk during WWII.

"My father's brother and his wife offered to take me to fill the void left by their son who had just died and who had been about my age. My sisters were taken in by my mother's sister, a Mother Superior of a convent school for girls. My father and my brother moved nearer to Boston where my father worked as a prison guard. In those days, it was the custom of widowed fathers to hire a live-in housekeeper to maintain the household and do the cooking while the father raised the children to the best of his ability.

"Meanwhile, I adapted to life with my new 'parents.' Not much distance separated me from my brothers, and as for my sisters, although they were boarders at the school, they came home very frequently so all of us could spend a great deal of time together.

"As Somerville, Mass was my new address, I went there right through high school. I graduated in 1931, at the height of the world-wide Great Depression. There were no 'real' jobs to be had, even for college graduates. We took what we could find and we were happy enough.

"After my military discharge in 1945, I decided to take advantage of the US Government GI Bill of Rights which provided a generous stipend toward a college degree. I was 36 at the time. It was the beginning of one of the happiest periods of my life.

"I thoroughly enjoyed walking along the Charles River from Beacon Hill where I lived to the campus of BU about 3 miles. I thought to myself 'Here I am walking to school, thirty years after the first time.' After 12 years of taking courses at night school, I graduated from Boston University at the age of 48.

"Every student takes a few elective courses to balance the required ones. My favorite was *Six Great British Writers*. It was one I'll never forget. To this day I remember our professor made us dig for the meat in these authors' works. We received a great lesson in persistence in deciphering the prose of James Joyce's *Portrait of the Artist as a Young Man* and the complexities of murky *Macbeth*. The other authors – Virginia Woolf, Thomas Hardey, and H.G. Wells – were equally challenging.

"As for my new position in the State House, I found myself a Field Accountant in the Office of the Comptroller of The Commonwealth of MA, meaning 'State.'

"Of all the aspects of my job, I enjoyed teaching the most. The main thrust of my work was to respond to requests for help, accounting wise, from the accountants in various state facilities, such as hospitals, prisons, colleges, and universities."

This ends my father's words.

A few years ago, someone asked my sister Kate what words she would use to describe my father in three words. A few days later, when Kate and I were talking, she asked me what adjectives I would use. Without hesitation, I answered: "Kind, gentle, intelligent."

She said: "Those are the exact words that I picked."

At this time, I would like to share a few of the comments that some people shared in their sympathy cards:

The following was from a neighbor of my dad in Florida. "Dick was a gentleman in every sense. He was an intelligent, principled guy. I will remember him for a hundred good reasons. I just had to make known my high regard for your father. No reply is necessary."

A college friend of my sister, Kate wrote: "What a delight he always was….. a generous, happy, curious, loving soul."

A long-time friend of my father wrote: "Your father was a much-loved person, friend, neighbor, and gentleman. I feel honored to have known him. He was always so kind and helpful…such a fine, decent man. He will be missed by a lot of people he touched."

Besides reading, my father enjoyed crossword puzzles and traveling. Over the course of his lifetime, he traveled to over twenty-three countries. In doing so, he made many friends and stayed in touch with them over the years. Dad always said that he got his money's worth 3X over when he traveled:

1. In anticipation,
2. While he was there,
3. In recollection.

My dad attended BU night school for twelve years and graduated with his BA when he was 48 years old. I am also very proud of my dad's war service. He married my mother in October of 1941 and joined the Navy's Hospital Corps in 1942. Since the Marine Corps is also a corps of the Navy, and they did not have any medics, they used Navy hospital personnel and facilities and "Pharmacist Mates" as field medics. After Pharmacist Mate school he was sent to Camp Lejeune, a Marine training base in North Carolina. After this second "Basic Training" he was assigned to the 4th Marine Division. He received additional training with the Marines at Camp Pendleton in California. He saw very rough duty during his tour in the Pacific, but he rarely talked about it. He was Pharmacist Mate 1st Class when he received his Honorable Discharge from the Navy. I wish I had a photo of him in his dress uniform. I am so proud of and grateful to both my exceptional parents.

I would like to mention that my father was a very religious man with a deep abiding faith. He was devoted to the Rosary and prayed it daily. It would be very accurate to say that my father was a strong Christian and gentle man. I would like to end with the following words (author unknown):

"The tears that dampen our eyes in times of mourning are tears of homesickness, tears of longing for our loved ones. But, it is we who are away from home, not they. Death has been for them a doorway to an eternal home. They are still with us, lovingly and tenderly waiting for the day when we too, will enter the doorway of our eternal home. It is such a mistake to see death as separation and nothing more. For us who believe, death is a preparation for eternal union with those we love, in peace and joy."

AMEN

Phillip L. Pendergast

WOODS HOLE FLASHBACKS

Jim Lowey's Spa back in the 1950s:
Booths by the windows,
Soda fountain in the back,
Two pin-ball machines.

Eddie Swift's hardware store:
The unique, musty smell of ropes, twines, etc.
Thin gentleman, soft spoken.
He called pennies "Coppers."

Al's Barber Shop by the drawbridge:
The smell of his "Fu Fu juice." (Bay Rum?)
Two barber chairs.

Sullivan's (Sully's) Bake Shop:
That wonderful bakery smell,
Jelly doughnuts were very popular,
Sully's "Bakers Dozen."

Gertrude Whiting's Art Studio, next to Sully's:
World famous artist – compared to John Singer Sargent,
Smell of oil paints and canvases,
Oil painting of a local person often in her window.

Louis Tsiknes's grocery story:
Penny candy in a bin near the front door,
Fresh cut vegetables,
Louis in an apron,
Charlie Hatzikon at the register.

The original (authentic) Cap'n Kidd:
Red and white oil skin tablecloths,
Long bar with beautiful marble arm rest,
Drip candles in Chianti bottles.

Claudia Pendergast's Real Estate Office:
Lots of crank-out windows,
Sound of gravel when you pulled into the Naushon parking lot,
Western Union with paper message strips glued onto the paper,
The time I got a Silver Dollar when I delivered a telegram.

Walking from Park Street:
Thru' the wooded path,
Over the little creek bridge,
Through the ballpark,
To 9:00AM Sunday Mass at St. Joseph's,
Altar Boy for five years.

Ed Jaskin's Drug Store by the bridge:
Lemon and lime drinks at the soda fountain,
Great comic book section: Dick Tracy, Superman, Archie, etc.

Watching the Geodesic Dome being constructed next to the
    Nautilus Motor Inn:
Red and green triangular scraps of fiberglass scattered about on
    the ground.

Riding our bikes to the Webster Rose Garden:
Castle-like mansion with pink stucco and light blue trim,
The Blue Garden and perhaps – the Blue Rose?

The loud blare of the fog horn going off –
Just as you drove past by the lighthouse!

Edie Bruce's charming house and Art Gallery:
Two rockers on the front porch,
Beautiful rear yard right on Eel Pond,
Two guest cottages.

Eddie Swift's
hardware store

Louis
Grocery Store

Claudia Pendergast at her office

AFTERTHOUGHTS

I never actually intended to write this book. My original plan was just to jot down a few accounts of my youth to leave to my two sons and grandchildren. However, as time passed and I continued to recall these events, I found that my recollections were increasing, as were the number of pages. At that point, I decided that I would incorporate my memories into this memoir. I have tried to categorize these short pieces into some kind of rough format with a title for each specific recollection. My hope is that each reader will find some of these stories informative and, in some cases, amusing. My desire is that each of you may discover some interesting facts about Woods Hole and the way the life was back in the 1950s and 1960s.

The famous author Thomas Wolfe (1900-1938) once stated that "You cannot go home again," and he was correct. You cannot go back and re-live your past days over again. However, you can go back to the village of your youth for a visit. That is what I have attempted to do in this book. I returned to Woods Hole as I remembered it used to be. Luckily, I have a very good long-term memory. I was surprised at how much detail I was able to recall as noted in the acknowledgements. I was also fortunate to have had quite a few Woods Hole friends who assisted me with their own recollections.

One of the most amazing things that I discovered about

Woods Hole is that it is such a tiny village, yet it is so well known and world famous. Woods Hole only measures about 2.2 square miles in land area and is surrounded on three sides by water. However, Woods Hole is home to many scientific institutions: The Marine Biological Laboratory (MBL), The Woods Hole Oceanographic Institution (WHOI), Woods Hole Climate Research Center, The Woods Hole School of Science, and the Woods Hole Aquarium. According to a US Census estimate, the population of Woods Hole was only 816 soles in 2020. When I grew up there, during the 1950s and 1960s, one could buy a really nice house for $10,000 to $15,000. However, as of 2021, the Zillow home value index states that the median value of a home in Woods Hole now is at least $889,382. Unfortunately, now, most of the folks working in Woods Hole cannot afford to buy a house there. Sadly, some of those quaint old family homes have been torn down and replaced by tall "McMansions" so as to get a better water view.

As I concluded my writing, I was struck by just how lucky I was to have been born in 1944 and grown up during the post war years in such a beautiful and unique village as Woods Hole. Moreover, I was truly blessed to have had such loving and hard-working parents, both of whom put such a high premium on education.

My wife, Gail, and I celebrated our 52nd anniversary this past August. We have two fine sons and two wonderful grandchildren. We have had many wonderful retirement years and have been able to travel a lot. We have had many great adventures. What more could a man hope or wish for? I have had a wonderful life and realize that I have been truly blessed.

Some Park Street Kids, 1952
Me on far right, my sister Claudia (Kate) in the center
Pendergast Family Photo

Some teenage friends in 1956
Ben Mixter on left, Chick Mixter on right, Steve Bray kneeling at top
Photo credit: Ben Mixter

ACKNOWLEDGEMENTS

I would like to take a minute to thank all the folks who contributed to my writing of this memoir. First I wish to thank my old Woods Hole friends who grew up with me back in the 1950s and 1960s: Stephen Bray, Ben Mixter, my sister Claudia Pendergast Dion, Greg Lehy, Donny Lehy, Diane Lehy Hoss, Noni Schleicher Davies, and Bob Thaler, my college roommate who spent many days in Woods Hole in the 1960s. Also thanks to Susan Fletcher Witzell for her input and thoughts.

I wish to give a special thank you to my long-time friend Bill Anderson who spent countless hours typing my story into his computer in preparation for presenting the draft to my editor, Stephanie Blackman, who carefully edited and formatted this book. I would be lost without her creativity and diligent efforts. This is the second book of mine that she has edited. She is the best.

Lastly, I would like to thank Gail, my wife of fifty-two years, who patiently listened to my Woods Hole recollections over and over again as I read them to her for her input. At this point she has learned more about Woods Hole than she ever wanted to know. She is even happier than I am that this memoir is completed.

I apologize if I have accidently omitted the name of anyone else who has helped me. I am glad that you have